Life's Scenic Lookout

A Sabbatical Story

ANDY PANG

© Copyright 2006 Andy Pang
All rights reserved. No part of this publication may be reproduced, stored in a retrieval system, or transmitted, in any form or by any means, electronic, mechanical, photocopying, recording, or otherwise, without the written prior permission of the author.

Note for Librarians: A cataloguing record for this book is available from Library and Archives Canada at www.collectionscanada.ca/amicus/index-e.html
ISBN 1-4120-8689-2

Printed in Victoria, BC, Canada. Printed on paper with minimum 30% recycled fibre. Trafford's print shop runs on "green energy" from solar, wind and other environmentally-friendly power sources.

TRAFFORD
PUBLISHING

Offices in Canada, USA, Ireland and UK

Book sales for North America and international:
Trafford Publishing, 6E–2333 Government St.,
Victoria, BC V8T 4P4 CANADA
phone 250 383 6864 (toll-free 1 888 232 4444)
fax 250 383 6804; email to orders@trafford.com

Book sales in Europe:
Trafford Publishing (UK) Limited, 9 Park End Street, 2nd Floor
Oxford, UK OX1 1HH UNITED KINGDOM
phone 44 (0)1865 722 113 (local rate 0845 230 9601)
facsimile 44 (0)1865 722 868; info.uk@trafford.com

Order online at:
trafford.com/06-0445

10 9 8 7 6 5 4 3 2

FOREWORD

In celebrating my 40th birthday, I took a year-long sabbatical to fulfill some dreams. A website – andypang.com – was created to document my experience during the year. This book collects the journal entries that appeared on the website. As a result, this is meant to be read as a journal rather than as a story book of one coherent theme.

A few years ago, I came to the realization that my life had been quite a blessing and that I would like to share this blessing with those who are less fortunate. Hence, the idea of a sabbatical was born. It was the best birthday gift I could have imagined for myself. There was no specific day-to-day plan as to how the year would be spent, lest it would feel too much like work. Basically, my intention was to spend approximately half of the time working with charitable organizations in Latin America - mainly in Costa Rica - while the rest of the time I would spend traveling and learning things that had always interested me. Along the way, I hoped to acquire a higher level of fluency in the Spanish language, to foster some new friendships and to gain a better understanding of the Latino culture, and myself.

I hope you find following the journey enjoyable. Comments are much appreciated and they may be directed to andypang@usa.com.

TO

All my English teachers

CONTENTS

1. How Did It Happen? 9
2. Updates From The Ultimate Concrete Jungle - Hong Kong 11
3. Farewell Hong Kong 14
4. Greetings From London, England 17
5. This Is No Vacation 20
6. Crumbs Of My Thoughts - London I 24
7. Crumbs Of My Thoughts - London II 27
8. From England To Denmark 30
9. Denmark - My Favorite Country 33
10. R & R In Denmark 36
11. Dallas For A Party 40
12. Hola! Welcome To Costa Rica 42
13. Panama For Christmas Part I 46
14. Panama For Christmas Part II 51
15. First Trip Of 2005 - Puerto Viejo 53
16. Reality As I Know It 56
17. At Home In Costa Rica I 60
18. Moving About In Greater San Jose 63
19. Extra! 68
20. Life's Guarantee And Surprise 74
21. At Home In Costa Rica II 76
22. Thoughts From Semana Santa (Holy Week) 80
23. Tico Life I 82
24. I Worry About You?! 86
25. Tico Education System 89
26. Medical Week 93
27. Notes From Dallas 95
28. Crossing The Big Pond Again 98
29. Transatlantic I: Aboard MS Lirica 100
30. Transatlantic II: Caribbean Ports of Call 104
31. Transatlantic III: Life On Board 108
32. Transatlantic IV: Upstairs Downstairs 113
33. Transatlantic V: Funchal - Paradise Discovered 117
34. Transatlantic VI: Mediterranean Ports Of Call 120
35. Transatlantic VII: Conclusion 123
36. Last Leg In Costa Rica 127
37. Children's Day Camp 131
38. A Walk In The Wild - Part I 134

39. A Walk In The Wild - Part II ········· 138
40. Update On Work & Puerto Viejo Revisited ········· 142
41. Tico Sex & Gender ········· 145
42. Tico Tele-Communications ········· 149
43. Tico Life II ········· 153
44. Pianoforte – My First Love ········· 156
45. My Fear Of Working With Children ········· 159
46. Tico Life III ········· 162
47. There's No Banquet That Doesn't End! ········· 166
48. Hong Kong: Homebound, Or Just Visiting? ········· 170
49. Fragrant Harbor I ········· 172
50. Fragrant Harbor II - Medical Practices ········· 176
51. Hangzhou, China - A City For Poets ········· 179
52. Other Observations In China ········· 183
53. Follow-up To Previous Entry ········· 187
54. Fragrant Harbor III - Education ········· 189
55. Fragrant Harbor IV - Katrina Talk ········· 192
56. Fragrant Harbor V - Public Transportation ········· 195
57. The Fat Lady Has Sung ········· 199
58. Epilogue ········· 204

1. How Did It Happen?

October 1, 2004 - Dallas, Texas, USA

After the idea of a sabbatical came to mind a few years ago, I went on a mission trip as an interpreter with my church to the Dominican Republic for a week in 2003. My main purpose for that trip was to confirm if I would really enjoy working with disadvantaged children. As you may recall, I reported in last year's newsletter that for the first time in my life I saw God in those children's faces. When I returned to the States, I started planning the sabbatical.

I researched organizations where I could be of service and educated myself how to proceed with the dream. There are many non-profit organizations that match volunteers with institutions throughout the world. Most of such services come with a hefty price tag - about $5,000 for two to three months. The fees charged - what I call "shipping and handling" - normally cover room and board, airline tickets, insurance, and field support. These programs target younger people, as well as older, who have little experience living overseas, who are not conversant with the language spoken in the host country, and who, most important of all, do not have a lot of time and flexibility to make plans of such a nature.

After much consideration, I, as a middle-aged man, decided to go it alone and create my own plan. It took me no time to realize the value of the above-mentioned organizations. Since I do have the time and flexibility, I am, to quote our 43rd president, "steadfast" in my resolve. Let's just hope that my resolve is not the result of being stubborn. This is starting to sound like an article written in an election year!

In April, I asked for a year off from my job and the request was subsequently granted. It is important to note here that I enjoy my job tremendously. The people with whom I worked in my last project would concur, I trust, that I had so much fun with my job that I am borderline insane. What it means is that I am not taking a break from my job because I am tired of it. Rather, I want to experience something that my current job does not offer and that money alone cannot buy – hence the name of this book and the website: Life's Scenic Lookout. This is a detour of life's journey taken on purpose. It is all positive and, at the moment, I fully intend to resume my job in October 2005.

I mapped out on paper a preliminary plan and proceeded to make it happen. The first lesson I learned is that this planning is a very lonely process. While I have read many people's accounts of their experiences on such a journey, I do not know anyone first-hand in this regard. During this process, I drew on my background as a travel agent frequently, and, whenever I had cold feet, I would look back to those fearless days when I first came to Texas as a naive college student. More so than ever, this journey itself, rather than the destination, is what really matters.

I rented a 10'x10' storage space where all my earthly possessions would reside for the year. A dear pianist friend of mine, Cheryl, kindly agreed to keep my piano for the period. My neighbors surely would not miss my practicing! I would literally live out of a suitcase, a roller-on, and a backpack for the next twelve months. This was not going to be a glamorous year for Andy.

Walkins, one of my best friends from high school, is getting married for the first time in October in Hong Kong. Of course, I would not miss the wedding banquet for the world, which ensues, incidentally, that the sabbatical starts with a visit to my roots and then onto a month long course of CELTA (Certificate of English Language Teaching to Adults) at International House in London, England. At the conclusion of the course, I will hop over to Grenaa, Denmark, to spend a few days with my Danish family before crossing the big pond. After that, all preparation will be done and I will head south to Costa Rica and start the core part of the sabbatical at the beginning of December.

Maintaining and updating this website is going to be a real test of my perseverance. I suppose only time can tell. Now I need to go purge and pack.

2. Updates From The Ultimate Concrete Jungle - Hong Kong

October 14, 2004 - Hong Kong, China

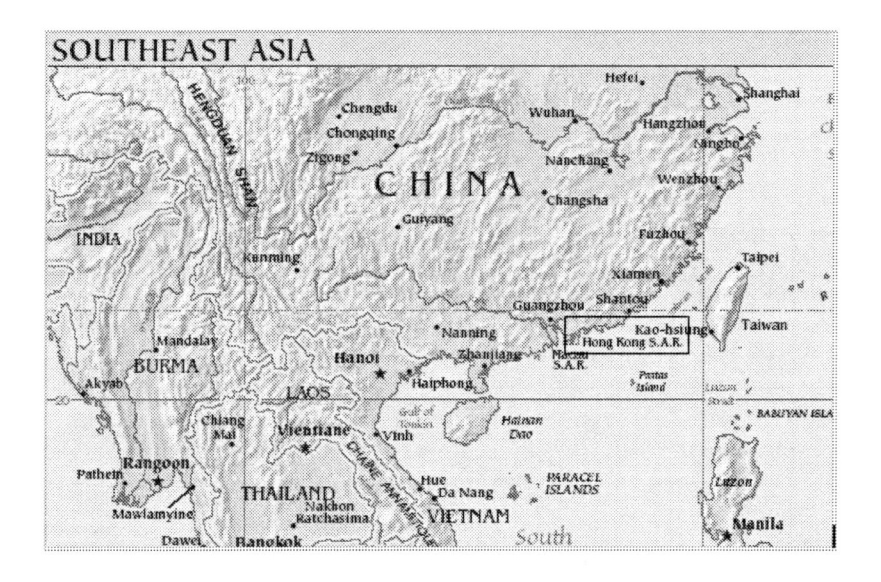

The Ultimate Concrete Jungle - Hong Kong

Hong Kong occupies a land mass of 1,103 square kilometers (426 square miles), 40% of which is reserved for country park or conservation areas. Simply put, its 7 million plus inhabitants live in 660 km² or 255 m². There is nowhere to go but up. The residential buildings are now taller than ever, with new ones reaching an average of 60 stories each. The highest residential building in town that I know of is a whopping 80 stories high. It offers a balcony with a glass railing on the waterfront. I say they can keep that balcony and I pray that the elevators never go out of service.

Daisy & Walkins' Wedding - Saturday, October 9, 2004

It was my first Chinese wedding banquet since 1997 and I enjoyed it tremendously - seeing my buddy getting married and meeting old school friends, some of whom I had not seen for 20 years. For my non-Chinese friends' sake, it is worth describing a Chinese wedding.

Our custom places more importance on the banquet than the wedding ceremony itself, especially if the wedding ceremony is a civil one taking place at a Marriage Registry in the city hall.

As in every Chinese wedding banquet, there was no dancing at my friend's wedding. The guests arrived at the hotel as early as 5pm and they gambled. That's right. The guests entertained themselves by playing mahjong. Some 10 tables were set up in the corner of the function room for this purpose. Meanwhile, the bride (sometimes together with the groom) served tea to the elders of the family; in return, the couple was presented with a red packet filled with cash or some jewelry as a token of the blessing of their marriage.

While the culture is changing fast in Hong Kong, a tradition that I appreciate very much remains, presumably for its practicality. When I arrived at the hotel, I, like every guest, presented to Walkins a red packet with my cash gift inside. My friends told me the prevalent rate: about US$65 for the wedding from a single attendant. This helps to defray the cost of the 10-course sit-down dinner and what-nots. More importantly, it saves everyone the trouble of coming up with an appropriate gift, in terms of both price and taste.

One Country, Two Systems

I am often asked by my friends who are not familiar with the handover of Hong Kong to China about this subject. In a nutshell, there is still a border between Hong Kong and the Mainland and the Mainlanders require special permits to enter Hong Kong. Recently, regulations were relaxed tremendously to make it easier for Canton residents to come to Hong Kong to spread their new wealth. Case in point, I read in the paper that a woman came to Hong Kong with her son during the National Day holiday week (Oct 1) and bought two new condos, for an impressive US$1.3 million. The Chinese shoppers usually come for the quality and authenticity of the products. Because Hong Kong is heavily dependent on the tourism money from the *comrades* from the other side, I am not sure if this border will last 50 years, as intended in the One Country Two Systems clause, which brings me back to my story.

There are a lot of cross border marriages, mainly with the groom in Hong Kong and the bride on the Mainland. Depending on where the bride holds her residence, it can take up to 7 years, on the average, before she can legally migrate to Hong Kong to join her husband (just in time to fix the 7 year itch?!!) This rule does not seem to apply to people holding other passports. Daisy happens to live in China; Walkins has an Australian passport. If they should want to live together sooner and Walkins should keep his job in Hong Kong, the *shortcut* is actually for Daisy to move to Australia and obtain her Australian passport through marriage to Walkins. It takes 2 years or so. She can then join him in Hong Kong as an Australian. I need to pitch this to Walkins before I leave.

Then I Got Sick

I felt the onset of the flu Sunday and did not feel up to going out to rub shoulders with the 7 million people. So I stayed home and indulged myself with *The Da Vinci Code*. All was not lost as this book is a definite page turner.

Currently, Hong Kong is obsessed with being slim. It is hard to imagine but there are even more commercials for this industry in Hong Kong than there are in the US. Considering how slim most people already ARE and considering that these same people still want to lose more, I have renewed respect for the power of marketing.

It is a hazard for me to come to Hong Kong - every gathering is done around food - and lots of it, good food too. My friends and family make sure I load up for the year ahead and feed me like there is no tomorrow. Meanwhile, they have no problem telling me, to my face, how FAT I have become over these years. As shocking as it may sound to foreign ears, this is not meant to be insulting. The trick of moving in and out of different cultures. I am no longer in Kansas......

More to come from Hong Kong.

3. Farewell Hong Kong

October 18, 2004 - Over the Pacific Ocean

Eleven days went by fast. Thanks to its over-booking policy, Cathay Pacific gave me a complimentary upgrade for my return flight from Hong Kong to Los Angeles as the flight was oversold. Such an upgrade affords me the comfort and leisure to write this last journal about the Hong Kong visit. Other than American Airlines' More Leg Room® service, economy class seats are not configured for people to use their laptop computers for an extended period, i.e. longer than 5 minutes!

Here are a few points of interest, I hope:

Land Sale

Please be reminded that these are my impressions and observations, which are HIGHLY subjective. I SHALL NOT be held responsible if you should decide to invest in Hong Kong real estate as a result of reading my thoughts. Real estate in Hong Kong plays a role that is fundamentally different. Early last week, the government auctioned two parcels of land and both were sold significantly above the expected price. Supposedly, this is an indicator that the housing price will go up again. That very evening, a lot of homes for sale were retracted. The sellers were waiting for the signs that might help them decide how much to raise the price. On the average, the prices went up 5% overnight. Such is the volatility of real estate. Then I saw one thing that I didn't remember seeing before. In America, when you read the real estate advertisements, you may see something like: Original Price, $200K, Reduced: $185K.

After the land sale in Hong Kong, I saw, multiple times, signs in real estate office windows: Original: $200K, Now: $215K. It signals to the prospective buyers that a profit is almost guaranteed. It makes perfect sense for this kind of market.

The Stress Of A Fast Paced Society

Things happen fast in Hong Kong. In such a competitive society, there is not much room to be wishy-washy in business. However, wealth has its side effects. In particular, child-rearing has become quite a challenge. I learned from my sister that a 14 year old jumped off a building recently, and succeeded in ending his life. The reason? Allegedly someone stole his weapons in an online game and he was too upset. Do keep in mind that I live mostly in an adults' world in the United States; therefore, I am not as aware of these things as I am in Hong Kong. I am sure raising a child in the States side is no walk in the park.

With so many distractions and contradictory values, seemingly more so than in America, the mere thought of raising a child in Hong Kong is too much for a wimp like me. And I am not alone. I went to a boys' high school and there were ten of us who were close during those formative years and we called ourselves Brothers Ten. I was the youngest, yet now all of us will be at least 40 by the end of this year. Of the ten, six are married and only two have children, two each. One other couple is planning to have children. All the others have decided to take our genes to our graves! I would imagine this is quite a relief to some, as even I myself cannot bear the thought of having an Andy Jr. terrorizing the other kids.

The future of Hong Kong will actually depend on the new immigrants from the Mainland. I always believe that the best way to control overpopulation is to make a society rich. All the wealthy countries have negative population growth. Immigration is what keeps these countries going, whether we like it or not, but that will be another journal entry down the road.

Every time I have gone home to visit in recent years, I have made sure to visit some of the elder relatives, especially my 80 year-old aunt. I have more uncles and aunts than I can count, but my closest aunt passed away 10 years ago. This remaining 80 year-old aunt is my prime source of information about the history of the family. Since most of their generation are illiterate (at least none of them seem to have the writer's genes), the knowledge of the family will be lost when they move on. Even though they are still around, I already start to miss my elderly relatives and my friends that I made during those tour-guiding years. They have all taught me so much. It saddens me to see how their love and wisdom are under-appreciated in our fast-paced society. Whew! It's the cabin pressure speaking.

I have only a few days to pack up the rest of the apartment while fighting the jetlag and then, on Friday, head to London for the CELTA course in International House London. Next entry will probably come from London.

4. Greetings From London, England

October 31, 2004 - London, England

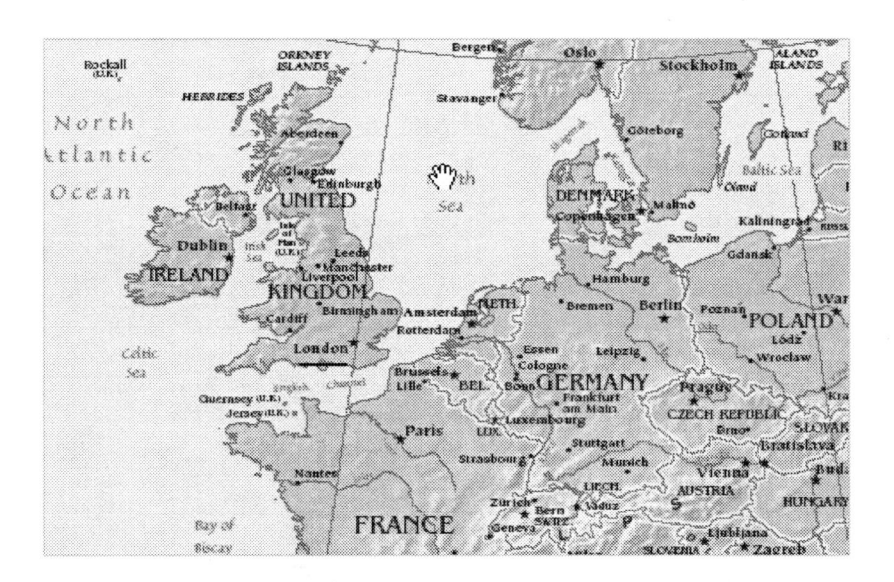

Those Dallas Days Between Hong Kong & London

When I got back to Dallas from Hong Kong, I worked on packing the apartment (part 2) and canceling my phone, utility and other such services. I got home Monday morning at 6am and left Friday at 2:30pm. I packed and packed, then I packed some more, and slept maybe for 10 hours altogether. I don't know where that junk hid in the 600 sq. ft. apartment. At one point, I wondered if the 10'x10' storage was going to be big enough. You can see what it looks like in the Galleries section on the web site. I did not have any time to spare. I turned in the apartment key and went to the airport, with the three bags, for my British Airways flight to London Gatwick Airport. No matter where I go in the next year, this is all I can carry. It's been working out so far.

If I had to do this again (someone has to twist my arm, really), I would keep everything in the apartment and sublease it to someone who has little or no furniture.

Arriving In London - Lugging The Bags All The Way To The House

The Gatwick Airport is located to the south, quite far away from the city. It would have bankrupted me if I had taken a cab to my host family. With those three bags, I took the Gatwick Express to the Victoria Station, then changed to the tube (subway) using two different lines. Being an older city, London is not made for people who are handicapped, or for those with heavy luggage. Escalators are available only after you have gone to the lobby/booking hall/concourse level. This is the case throughout London. Only a handful of stations are currently fitted for handicap access. Seeing the people negotiating the THOUSANDS (with bags, it feels like it) of steps with their canes or luggage is not a pretty sight.

It was a pretty cool day when I arrived, about 50 degrees. With the wind and rain, everyone dressed appropriately for the weather. It was comic that I was wearing only a shirt and sweating as if I were in a sauna while others around me in the tube car were wearing turtle neck sweaters, thick jackets and scarves. The theme repeated itself for a few days. The ventilation is generally horrible in London. After walking to the subway station, I would normally be quite warm already. Once I stepped inside the tube, I started to sweat. The condition doesn't always allow for enough room to take off your coat. Besides, nobody seems to feel the need to do so, and I normally just suffer quietly. I later learned to take off my coat before boarding the train.

Family Stay

I have chosen to have the school arrange homestay for me. This service is provided for students from other countries who come to study English in London. The homestay program allows students a window through which to see how the English live on a daily basis. More importantly, it gives them more opportunities to practice their English outside the classroom.

I have chosen the same service, more for cost reasons than for practicing my English. My family has a very big house. The children are grown, so they take in students to keep the house lively. The father is of Polish origin and he came to live in England after he was released from the concentration camp in—what was some 60 years ago—Czechoslovakia. The mother is of German origin though she was actually born in Israel. She came to England to study English many years ago and met her husband by chance. They both speak very good English. You almost can't tell that they aren't English. Most importantly, they are both extremely nice to the students living with them.

They can take in as many as 7 students at a time. Right now there are three: me, a 16 year boy from Shanghai, and a young woman from Lebanon. Normally there would be a Japanese person or two, but not this time. We all study at the same school. The woman from Lebanon has the best idea though. Her English is already quite good as she was educated at American University in Beirut. She signed up for Business English and Advanced English. This is her first visit to Europe and she is here more for vacation than for learning English. She has a relatively less expensive place to stay and has a natural avenue to meet people. It is a great idea.

Breakfast (cereal, toast) is provided every day. I signed up only for 4 dinners a week (Monday-Thursday) and have the weekend meals on my own. Laundry is provided once a week. This arrangement costs me 540 pounds (about $900) for the 4 weeks. The house is 8 subway stops away, or 45 minutes door-to-door between the school and the house. Not bad for London. I also found a great (read good & cheap) Chinese restaurant in Camden Town and have been a regular on the weekends.

Walk, Walk, Walk

Here, my newly discovered Internet Shop is 15 minutes from the house on foot. There are many internet cafes in and around the city. However, so far, this is the only one that allows me to dock my laptop, but it costs $4 an hour. Using their computers, however, is only half the price! Back in Dallas, this is definitely driving distance. In addition to my walk between the station and the house, and then between the station and the school, the building where my class is held is a five story building without elevators. As a result of all this walking, usually with a rather heavy book bag, the normal condition of my legs is soar!

5. This Is No Vacation

November 5, 2004 - London, England

The School

The International House London is a good size language school. A lot of foreigners come here to learn English. There is evidence that Chinese students will take over as the largest nationality represented on campus soon. In addition to English, a variety of modern languages, including Japanese and Chinese, are being taught here. Besides teaching languages, the School also provides a large number of opportunities for training in English teaching and other major European languages.

There is a full service cafeteria in the school, half of which is designated non-smoking. Unless you put up walls, this so-called smoking and non-smoking section is really a joke as you can still smell the smoke from far away, owing largely to the poor ventilation. I have grown rather allergic to smoking. I have been suffering from quite a bad sore throat since the third day in school. This has proven to be quite a problem as I HAVE TO teach at least 2 lessons a week.

The School has the slowest 'high speed' internet connection. It is no better than dial-up. No kidding. The computer lab is also the best sealed room I have ever been in. It is always at the boiling point no matter how cool it is outside. But I am not complaining. It DOES offer free access to the internet. An internet cafe charges an average of $2 an hour. I thought about signing up for T-Mobile Hotspot for just one month but then decided against it after I experienced the first week in the course.

The Training Course Itself

This is a four-week intensive course. The keyword here is "intensive." We have lectures from 9am to noon, and then we have to teach REAL students from 1-3pm, followed by review until about 4pm. In order to get the Cambridge certificate, we have to write four papers in a month and teach 8 classes at 3 different levels. It doesn't sound like a lot on paper, but it is WORK. I have taught 4 classes so far. The night before each class, I stayed up until 1 or 2am to write the lesson plan and prepare myself.

To show you the size of the school, there are 3 teacher training classes taking place simultaneously, with 15 trainees in each. In my class, there are 11 British students (9 English,1 Cypriot, 1 Irish), 1 Australian, 1 Egyptian, 1 Taiwanese, and me. Our ages range from the age of fresh college graduates to the late fifties. The class is divided into 3 groups of 5 for teaching practice purposes, with each group containing one of the 3 non-native speakers. As part of the lesson plan, we have to state the aim of the lesson as well as our personal aims. In my first lesson, I stated my personal aim: "Not to feel inadequate teaching in front of my English colleagues." I must confess that it was intimidating trying to teach English when you are being evaluated by your tutor and being observed by other native speakers. But it all ended up really well, and to my surprise, I actually didn't notice any feelings of inadequacy. Well, wait until I have to teach prepositions!

In a stressful situation, the group dynamics can become peculiar. Fortunately, we all have chosen to help one another out instead of cutting one another's throat. I have met some really nice people in this class.

My first practice group is for the pre-advanced students. How it works is that the school advertises to the foreign students, stating that they can take 2 hours of free English lessons in the afternoon from the teacher trainees. So, the majority of *my* students are currently taking lessons from other experienced teachers in the morning. The class is also offered to immigrants (some maybe refugees) for free. On top of that, anyone else can sign up for the class for a nominal fee. This turns out to be very helpful for trainees like us because the students are as motivated to learn as the trainees are to teach.

My first class is made up of 14 students of the following nationalities: Spanish, Angolese, Italian, Cuban, French, Turkish, Iran Kurdish, Japanese, Polish & Ukrainian. The school is quite a little United Nations! Picture this. These people are sitting in a classroom in London learning English from a Hong Kong Chinese individual who lives in Texas. A lot of hilarious things can happen. Fortunately, they are all very "lovely," as the Brits call it, and I did not run into any problem in this potentially awkward situation.

Luck would have it that my first assigned lesson was to teach the difference between British and American English. It took place on day 4 of the course. Having learned British English growing up in Hong Kong and having lived in the US for 15 years gave me a distinct advantage. Part of the lesson was to listen to conversations in British and American English. While I was playing the tape, it dawned on me that the speakers were not Americans. The publisher was too cheap to hire "real" Americans for that portion of the tape. Instead, they had some Brits fake American accents. I didn't tell the students - no need to complicate my lesson unnecessarily, but I thought it was hilarious.

At the beginning of the second week, I felt really glad that I chose to take this class before going to teach in Costa Rica. I had no idea how much work it is to teach, nor how to teach English, really. To teach a 40-minute lesson, it takes each of us, on the average, 6 to 8 hours to prepare for the lesson. We have to think about how to present the language, and then research how that particular tense or sentence structure works thoroughly. For instance, I never really thought about the difference between "I'll call you tomorrow" and "I'm going to call you tomorrow." This is a teaching course, not a grammar course for us. So, we have to research all of these on our own, depending on what is to be covered in our respective lessons.

I have since moved to my next level of teaching practice - pre-intermediate. It all works the same, except this time, there are 18 students registered, representing – *are you ready?* here we go:

Afghanistan, China, Japan, Egypt, Poland, France, Italy, Argentina, Myanmar (formerly Burma), Mexico, Turkey, Lithuania, Russia, Angola and Somalia

Anyway, this is really hard work. This also explains why I have been so tardy in updating the journal. I only sleep 4-6 hours a night during the week, depending on whether a paper is due or whether I have to teach the following day. But this has been great fun and it has been challenging. Taking this course is also one of the smartest decisions I have made. Anyone who has known me for any duration would have heard that I have wanted to be a teacher all my life. While I am fulfilling my lifelong dream to study in England, now I know first-hand what exactly I have been missing, and I can die without any regrets! Finally.

An Accidental Fan Of Starbucks

I am not a big fan of Starbucks in the US. But I love them here. For one, they are everywhere. It's also one of the few places that I can spend hours without subjecting myself to second hand smoke as they do not allow smoking in their shops. Their justification? Smoking will adversely affect the taste of their coffee. So, I bought a small mocha for $5 (thanks to Dave Stewart for introducing me to this drink) and am now sitting here for hours writing on my computer on the weekend. Signing off from Starbucks at Leicester Square (aka the theater district).

6. Crumbs Of My Thoughts - London I

November 19, 2004 - London, England

Since I am catching up with the journal, the stories here follow no particular timeline.

An Update On The CELTA Course

Alas! It's over. How the month went by was beyond me. The only things outside of this course that I can remember are: the US Presidential Election, the derailment of a Plymouth-bound train from Paddington, London, and the death of Yasser Arafat. Now that I get to slow down a bit and think about the course, it feels very much like a "go-live" weekend that has lasted 4 weeks (this is jargon for the computer industry folks).

My last teaching practice group was for the beginning level. The students were just as eager to learn as the ones in the other levels. The problem was ME. For one, as you can imagine, it's very difficult for me to talk slowly enough for most people. Then, one has to use very simple language. All phrasal verbs, for instance "fed up," are to be avoided at all cost. It is exhausting trying to "speak with the brakes on" while "trying to reduce the language level." I was wiped out after teaching each of the 60-minute lessons. But it's also very satisfying when the students hang on to every single word we utter. How much they truly understand is a different story. This is by far the most difficult level to teach. You have to be really creative as verbal communication tools are very limited at this level.

For some reasons unbeknown to me, the class of 23 was made up of quite a few Brazilians. There were also Chinese, Turkish, Lebanese, Iraqi, Bolivian, Colombian, Peruvian, Polish, Congolese, Spanish, Afghan and Yemeni students. By now you should be able to get a picture of the composition of the nationalities. There is a pattern there somewhere.

I have fortunately passed all the teaching practices and the written assignments. The school mails the preliminary course results the week after the course. It doesn't matter anymore really. It has been a fascinating and thrilling experience. And I look forward to sleeping the weekend away in Denmark.

A Day Out On The Thames And At The Royal Observatory

Winter finally arrived in the UK last Friday night (Nov 12). Along came two beautiful days over the weekend. I took advantage of the good weather on Saturday (Nov 13) by taking a cruise down the Thames from Westminster to Greenwich. Including the stop at St. Katherine's Pier (by Tower Bridge), the journey took about an hour. It was a perfect day for the journey, albeit a bit cold.

I learned of Greenwich Mean Time when I was a child in Hong Kong and was always interested in visiting the very spot where GMT was based. Somehow I failed to do so during the previous visits to London. So, my visit to Greenwich was easily one of the highlights of my stay in London this time.

A bit of education here, in case you are interested. I could remember this wrong, so read this with a grain of salt. The word "mean" comes from the fact that the sun dials used to measure time in the old days had a margin of error of up to 16 minutes in the course of a year. The mean time was literally the "adjusted time," and each city now has its own mean time. The need to standardize time resulted from the establishment of national rail services. The same was also said to be true in the US. The GMT is now the official international time.

The Royal Observatory in Greenwich was founded by King Charles II in 1675. The Flamsteed House was designed by Christopher Wren (the same gentleman who designed St. Paul's Cathedral) as a home for the Astronomer Royal. The Prime Meridian at Longitude 0º was fixed here in 1884, and it is possible to stand astride this line with one foot in the Western and the other in the Eastern hemispheres simultaneously. Admission to the museum is free and well worth the time.

The UK Telephone System

A few points about the UK telephone system. Calling a mobile (cellular) phone costs (quite a bit) more than calling a land line. The calling party pays for the call; it's completely free to the receiving party. This really deters the direct marketing calls. A charge applies when you use a land line to call another land line in your local area, a bit less than 2 cents per minute. This is in addition to the fixed charge for the land line. If you have a dial-up internet connection, connecting to your internet provider's local number costs more than calling a local phone number. And you have to pay per minute. Using a mobile phone to call another mobile phone incurs different charges depending on whether the receiving party uses the same carrier. The differences can be substantial, especially if you have a Pay As You Go plan.

It took me a while to learn all these pieces of information. Compared with the UK, the US has a much simpler system, which, in my opinion, favors the users rather than the telephone companies. So, with such complicated and tiered charges, I conclude that the UK phone companies, while subject to heavy competition, are faring better than their US counterparts. I say they are smarter yet are worse for the customers though.

Doors Everywhere

If you are into slamming doors, you are in paradise in England. Every room in the house where I live has a door. The living room can be completely sealed off. So can the dining room, the kitchen, and the breakfast nook. In fact, you can get inside a house and only find yourself locked in the hallway. This is true in many of the homes I have visited. I asked the landlord why this is the case and he was not sure. My only logical conclusion for this is that they can separate the children from the adults, as well as women from the men, etc. (oops, reading too much Jane Austen). Maybe it is just for heating purposes. Why heat up the whole house if everyone can be confined in the living room or drawing room?

By the way, every door has a key to it. The beauty of the system is that if a thief breaks into the house, say from the kitchen window, he will find himself locked in the kitchen, without access to the rest of the house.

7. Crumbs Of My Thoughts - London II

November 20, 2004 - London, England

The Cars Have Gotten Bigger

I always remember the cars in England being very small. What Mr. Bean (from the TV program) drives was what I saw a lot in the past. This time around, I found the cars have grown in size. With gasoline at about $6 a gallon, I would have a minor heart attack every time I filled up.

Fortunately, there exists this thing called a "travel card." I bought a travel card for about $142, which allowed me unlimited travel within zones 1 and 2 for a month using the tube (subway), as well as the bus and light rail systems. Everything is so expensive, but this is one of the few things that I found affordable. And when I felt like it, I hopped on the double deck bus and got a free tour of the city (wherever that route might take me).

By the way, the London Underground (aka The Tube) has quite comprehensive coverage. As a result, the route map requires some training to read. If you want to feel what it looks like to a non-English speaker, this is what you can do. Next time when you cook spaghetti, take out 50 strands or so and put them on a plate randomly. That's what the tube map looks like; except it's more colorful on the tube map than your plate of spaghetti.

London Is Expensive

EVERYTHING is expensive in London. When I first looked at the prices, I didn't think much of them. The numbers themselves are about the same as US prices. When I realized that Sterling Pounds were 85% more expensive than US Dollars, the shock never left me.

A cup of regular coffee at Starbucks costs more than $3. Once, I went to Burger King for a whopper value meal, and the till showed 4.62 pounds. When I sat down to eat and converted the price to US dollars, I savored every single french fry. The meal was a whopper all right. It carried a whopping $8.5 price tag. Thank goodness I didn't super-size it; I might have had to pawn the watch for that!

To further demonstrate, a pack of fags (cigarettes) from the vending machine costs 5.2 pounds, or $9.6. ALMOST TEN DOLLARS. This knowledge solved a puzzle for me and brought a question to mind at the same time. The question - the minimum hourly wage in London is 5 pounds. What came first? The price of ciggies or the minimum wage?

Londoners are quite trim when compared with the average American. Some of the men that I have seen in the tube are down right skinny or even look as if they are suffering from malnutrition. At first, I thought it was the result of exercise from walking. Remember the steps in the tube stations? Then I thought it was the smoking. Half of the package is covered with "Smoking Kills" using font size 36 (No, I didn't actually measure it!) So, I thought it was health-related. Smoking is less of a social taboo in the UK than it is in the US. Then I found the missing piece when I saw the price of ciggies for the first time. At almost $10 a pack, what smokers would still have money left for lunch??!!

The US Election

All I want to say is that the Europeans are very disappointed with the presidential election results. A survey was done in England and only 30% supported Bush and 70% supported Kerry.

Ban That Filth

When I first arrived in London, I saw this TV program called Ban That Filth. I think it was on Sunday night. Unfortunately, I never did catch that program again. The host of the program was an old lady. She was helped by two even older ladies who did the research on her behalf using the phone and TV guides.

The host lady informed the TV audience of the upcoming programs in the week that contained nudity (both male and female) and such. She showed the clips, and then the showing time and name of the show came on the screen. She seemed to get more of a kick out of those male clips. The two even-older ladies showed their facial disapproval from behind the desk, often times while they were (pretending to be?) on the phone. Then a big stamp of "Ban That Filth" covered the whole screen. The three of them reminded me of Sophia from Golden Girls. If you are not familiar with Sophia (how can you not be?), then think of the Church Lady from Saturday Night Life. This went on for a while. I was initially quite shocked by such a conservative movement in the UK. Then it dawned on me what was happening and I laughed until I cried.

Instead of promoting banning the "filth," they were ACTUALLY advertising them for the shows. I almost missed that sense of humor. And they chose three old ladies to do the show! It's really clever and funny. Well, you had to be there.

Starbucks Revisited

There is a big difference between the Starbucks here in London and the Starbucks in the US. First, if you have your coffee in the shop, you are served your coffee in a beaker (mug) instead of paper cups. It makes the experience more cozy. For the pastries, the eat-in price is roughly 20-25% higher than the takeaway price.

Farewell To The CELTA Class & Smoking Ban In 2008

On Thursday, the class went out to celebrate the conclusion of the course. We went to a pub close to the school and some of us stayed for almost 5 hours. This pub has a really high ceiling and good ventilation. I could even handle the smoke. A day earlier, to my astonishment, a law was passed by the Parliament to ban indoor smoking throughout England, effective 2008. This includes all restaurants and pubs. I don't know why it takes 4 years for the law to be in effect. That's minor though. What I can't wait to see is how the people in the city, be they Brits or foreigners, handle such a fundamental change in their daily lives. Incidentally, such a law is already in effect in Ireland nowadays. It shows that it can be done.

Anyway, we had a good time chatting about the "bloody" course experience and really getting to know one another for the first time. We had a good time and we vowed to stay in touch. We shall see. I hope we will.

Well, I am off to Denmark!

8. From England To Denmark

November 21, 2004 - Grenaa, Denmark

Looking Back On The Month In London

The purpose of including Denmark in the itinerary is mainly to visit old friends and have a bit of R&R. Now that I get to slow down, I realize that there were many thoughts that I meant to include but didn't in the previous entries.

I have been to London quite a few times in the last 18 years (more than 10 actually). However, this visit was very different. I felt more like a resident of the city than a tourist, albeit a short term one. The difference during this visit is that there was a very defined routine for the four weeks. I went to school every morning at about the same time, using the same subway route. When I started to recognize the faces in the tube and on the street, both on the way to the station and to the school, that's when this feeling that things were different came over me. This feeling deepened when, over a few occasions, I was, along with other commuters, subject to the frustration of the delay and malfunction of the underground trains.

Whenever I am in a foreign country, I love traveling by public transportation. This is when you really get to see (and smell) the people in close proximity. Observing the local people, and sometimes the other foreigners, is my favorite pastime. The London Underground publishes a daily newspaper called the Metro. It's free and widely available in the stations. And that's the paper most people read in the subway cars.

To prevent people from further littering the cars with loose paper from this newspaper (they already do so with drinks and other stuff), the publisher is smart enough to staple the paper together. So, it reads more like a pamphlet, though a thick one, than a regular newspaper. When people leave the subway cars, they usually leave the paper behind for other passengers who didn't pick one up from the station. It actually works out quite well.

London is my favorite big city. I don't know why but I really like London and I don't have nearly the same level of affection for New York City. The thing that I like most about London is that it feels very safe. Pick pocketing is a problem, but that's a problem in every big city. You feel quite safe even when you walk alone late at night. Besides, I love hearing all the different languages. You can do this in the buses and subway cars. I swear that all the world's languages are spoken in London.

In the train stations and subway stations, it's difficult to find trash cans. I think they had been removed when it was unstable in Northern Ireland quite a few years ago and bombs were placed in trash cans in the stations and in the city. In the airports, the ubiquitous red mailboxes are partially transparent so that one can see what items have been deposited.

Ryanair - Headache For The Established European Airlines

Ryanair is the Southwest Airlines of Europe, based at Stansted Airport outside of London. To say it's in London is a stretch; it's definitely closer to Cambridge. Fortunately, it's connected to Central London by an express train that takes only about 45 minutes. It's the European airline that reports the largest profit currently. In fact, I don't know who else reports a profit – Easyjet maybe. Ryanair is the airline I used to fly to Denmark this time. I used it a few years ago when SAS (Scandinavian Airlines Systems) discontinued its London/Aarhus service. I didn't have fond memories of Ryanair due to a cancelled flight, but I chose it again.

Fares in Ryanair can be unbelievably cheap. You can sometimes get a one-way ticket for a few dollars (but you still have to pay tax and airport fees, which will still amount to 30 dollars or so). Like Southwest Airlines, Ryanair flies an exclusive fleet of Boeing 737s (I am quite sure), it uses smaller airports that are further from town, and there is no seat assignment. That's about where the similarities end.

To expedite cleaning and, hence, turnaround time, the pockets of the seats have been removed and replaced with nets. The cleaning crew can see if there is any trash to remove without peeking into every pocket. For boarding and disembarking, they use both the front and back doors simultaneously. They really beat Southwest on that one! It's an absolute point-to-point carrier. Bags are only checked to the immediate destination.

Nothing is free onboard Ryanair. You have to BUY your soft drink and peanuts, should you want some. Once airborne, you feel more like being in a little moving mall. First comes the menu for the drinks and food - quite a choice for short haul flights, really. I think it's also done to make sure that there is no misunderstanding for the first time Ryanairers.

Everything is an advertising opportunity. The little piece of paper or cloth that airlines put on the headrests of the seats are used to advertise for Mars, the candy bar. Then there is the usual duty free shopping. I really think Ryanair is in the retail business rather than in transportation, like McDonald's is in real estate rather than in fast food. In the shopping catalog, other than your routine perfume and such, they also sell practical things such as toothpaste and tooth brush kits for 5 pounds sterling, or the price of a pack of cigarettes! When you see a barf bag (or sick bag) in the back pocket of an airliner, what do you see? A blank, mostly white, waterproof bag, right? In Ryanair, the barf bag is a dual purpose bag; in addition to its traditional purpose, it can also be used for sending your films in for developing. I took a picture of the bag when I realized what it was doing. Let's just hope that nobody sends in the wrong bag to the store.

Then they also sell train tickets on the plane, for the connection from Stansted Airport to Liverpool Street Station in Central London via the Stansted Express. They were also selling some raffle tickets, available only to adults, for a trip. I think that one was co-sponsored by the airline and the London Underground. The flight attendants were busy doing all these transactions and the flight only lasted an hour and 25 minutes!

I can't remember it all, but it was a sight. And I am not exaggerating, not in the least bit.

9. Denmark - My Favorite Country

November 24, 2004 - Grenaa, Denmark

The Kingdom Of Denmark

Denmark is the longest lasting continuous kingdom in the world. It has been my favorite country since 1986.

The place I visited is called Grenaa (the "aa" combination carries somewhat of an "o" sound, if you try to pronounce this place). It's a small harbor town of about 17,000 people tucked away in a quiet corner of Djursland, on the Jutland peninsula. I first came to this place in 1986 and have been in love with it ever since. It looks and feels like a scene out of a Hans Christian Andersen fairy tale.

How I Met My Danish Family

Most of my friends know that I have some Danish friends. Here's our story.

When I was a student in Hong Kong, I was fascinated by the English language and would talk to tourists whenever I could in order to supplement the few lessons that I got in school. In the summer of 1983, I was on a train on my way to town to meet a friend when I sat next to a group of four Europeans. I was reading Kramer vs. Kramer for a book report and had no intention of speaking to them. Then I noticed they weren't speaking English. The summer before, I took a French course and I tried to listen if they were speaking French. That's when our eyes met. They had their maps in their hands and obviously were trying to find out how to get to a certain place. We smiled at one another and we started to talk. That smile started a most fulfilling lifelong friendship that has crossed continents and oceans over the last eighteen years.

It ended up they were looking for the way back to their hotel and I was heading in the same general direction. So, I walked them to where they could find their way. When we were about to say goodbye, I asked them if they would like to come to my school's open-house day a few days later. We spent a whole day touring the city and visiting different schools - they were all teachers at that time. Ole and Vibeke, the father and mother, were on a 6-month round-the-world tour; Steen and Hanne, the son and then girlfriend (now wife), joined them for the Hong Kong and Japan portion. At the end of the day, we exchanged addresses and wrote to each other during the following years.

I went to visit them for the first time in Denmark in May 1986, my first trip out of Hong Kong and China. I was 21. That's when I met the rest of the family. Kasper, the artist who currently lives in London, was born three months before my visit. The family has since grown from 1 to 7 grandchildren in the last 18 years. That trip started my passion for travel. I worked for a travel agency at the time and got the ticket for 10% of the cost. The 17-day trip covered England, Denmark, and Bahrain (in the Middle East) and cost about US$240. I also learned how to travel with a small budget.

Grenaa is everything that Hong Kong is not. It was quite a cultural shock to be there the first time. I have never been to such a small town and such a tranquil place. Shops closed early during the week and remained closed for the weekend from early Saturday afternoon. They still do. There are no traffic jams; well, there is almost no traffic for that matter. The air is always clean. The houses are neat and painted in vibrant colors. It was also the first time I had a room to myself. Lots of unforgettable memories. At the end of the visit, when I got back on the SAS flight for London, I was so emotional that I was unable to eat and I refused dinner from the flight attendant. I wasn't sure if that would be the last time I would see the Hansens.

To my great fortune, between 1986 and 2004, I visited Denmark 6 times. Things have changed a little over the years. Denmark has taken in its share of refugees resulting from the wars in Bosnia. That injection of a different culture, mostly Muslim, is changing the homogeneous Danish culture.

My Danish Family

I am sure that my view of Denmark is very subjective as a result of my association with my Danish family. Besides, I am known as Andy Hansen Pang in Denmark so, of course, I am biased!

Please don't get the impression that all Danish families are as talented as mine. I have been assured that they are not your typical Danes, though they do carry on with many of the great traditions of this old kingdom. There are many musicians - vocal and instrumental artists, song/musical writers, published authors, gardeners, actors, and magicians, to name a few. For example, one of the Danish traditions during birthday parties is to write songs for the birthday boy/girl (mostly older people, I think) and sing them at the party. And my Danish family writes those songs. Danish is spoken by only about 5 million people on the planet; as a result, the teenagers speak an average of three languages - English and some other European languages, like German or French. They take English for three years in school and can speak it quite fluently already. My friends put on art exhibitions and puppet shows, and they make the puppets themselves. Of course, some of the stories are original too. In spite of this fury of activity, they are not workaholics by any means. Also worth mentioning is that nobody among the generations in this family smokes. This beats the odds in Europe big time. Whenever I am with them, I feel very under-achieving.

10. R & R In Denmark

November 25, 2004 - Grenaa, Denmark

Home To Denmark

I went to Denmark with one clear objective - to rest and visit with friends. On the whole, I spent a lot of time catching up with the family and talking about world affairs.

Ole and Vibeke met me at Tirstrup Airport on a cold morning and we went home for a smorrebrod lunch (open face sandwich). Steen, Hanne and Jonas (their son, daughter-in-law, and grandson) joined us. Kasper, the young artist who is living in England, is the older son of Steen and Hanne, whom I met back in Hong Kong in 1983 together with Vibeke and Ole. They live within walking distance from Vibeke & Ole up the hill. Smorrebrod is a typical Danish food. It is a sandwich with only one piece of bread (the bottom one). In this family, they use a lot of fish, but I suppose one can use beef if necessary. Since I like fish, it suited me really well. And I already miss the smorrebrod very much. However, I am still not used to eating herring pickles. Incidentally, the only other time I have heard the word "herring" being used is from a story told by Rose (one of the Golden Girls) on TV. Had it not been for Rose, I wouldn't even know that a herring is a kind of fish.

An Early Danish Christmas Meal

I was treated to a traditional Danish Christmas meal that night. Steen, Hanne and Jonas prepared quite a delicious meal. They told me that the windmill, which has been the town symbol for more than 100 years and is close to both houses of my friends, burned down last year. Fortunately, the town voted to rebuild it and it should be back completely in late December or early 2005. The town people can rent the place for functions, parties and exhibitions.

That same night Jonas and I spent some time playing piano. We took turns playing and while the adults finished up preparing the meal in the kitchen. He taught me quite a few useful things about how to play the chords. Unfortunately, my travel south of the boarder will not give me much access to a piano to practice what he has taught me.

Danish Tax Money At Work (Some Of It)

Jonas is twelve and has been taking piano lessons for three years. He has piano lessons once a week at his school after school. The government subsidizes such activities and there are many things to choose from. This is another reason I adore this country. They invest money where it matters. The people, for the most part, can see what their (very high) tax money is spent on.

Education is free all the way up to and including university. It's very competitive to get in, but if you are in, it's free and you get a small allowance from the government while you are studying. All medical services are free to the citizens. The roads are in good conditions. And so on. And so on.

Make no mistake, the government does make mistakes. However, from the view of a foreigner who visited for only a few days, it seems to me that they are doing more right than wrong.

My First Birthday Party Of 2004

Marie, Vibeke & Ole's daughter, and her family came to lunch Sunday. Amelie, Marie's daughter, sings in a choir that won the title of being the country's best choir recently. The choir just came back from Canada in October after sightseeing and performing. Alexander, the middle child, is good at football and chess - great combination since he can use his chess strategies to benefit his football games as a mid-field player. He just started learning English this year and our conversations were short as a result. Viktor, the youngest son, is eight. He and I communicated with smiles. He's fascinated with trains, planes and big machines in general. He has already read two Harry Potters (in Danish). Did I say he's only eight?

Steen's family was there as well. We had a wonderful assortment of smorrebrod. Now and then, they sang traditional Danish songs throughout the meal and I got updates on how the children were progressing in school and such. It's fascinating to hear how different the education system is in Denmark. I still don't understand the whole system. When one finishes 9th grade, then one sort of decides on a career before moving on to high school or gymnasium. Instead of proceeding with one's academic endeavors, one can attend technical schools to learn to be a carpenter, electrician, plumber, etc. Their approach is much more practical.

Two cakes were baked for the occasion - one with a Danish flag and the other with an American flag. I had a birthday song sung to me in Danish. It's quite a long version and sounded unmistakably Viking to my ears.

After the meal, we took a walk to see the windmill (under reconstruction) - mind you, it was about 1 or 2 degrees Celsius, or 33 to 35 Fahrenheit and windy. The Danes are used to these long and cold winters. In fact, as long as the ground is not icy or covered with snow, you will see people biking (more as a mode of transportation than a mode of exercise) all over the place. Vibeke and Ole went biking one morning, to my amazement, for an hour. And it was raining. No wonder they are so healthy.

Hair Cut

One of my concerns while traveling for a year was where to have my hair cut. In the last eight years, my hair was cut by the same person, Wendy, at Supercuts. She knew my hair and the cut was always fast and consistently satisfactory. When I worked in Holland for three months in 2001, I synchronized my flight home every 3 weeks with the haircut.

For people who have a full head of hair, they probably don't care as much. But if you have as little as I do, you can't afford mistakes or a bad cut. At my friends' recommendation, I went to see Inge in town as my haircut was way overdue. It was a really good haircut and I was more than satisfied. It was about US$30, double the price of my cut in the US. I just can't afford it every three weeks now that I no longer have an income!

Christmas Shopping

I went Christmas shopping with Vibeke & Ole in Aarhus, the second largest city in Denmark. It was a Wednesday afternoon and the shops were full of people in the afternoon. Remember that shops close at 6pm during the week and open only Saturday morning during the weekend. I think the late night shopping is on Thursday. It seems inconvenient at the beginning but I really like this system. Most people can have their weekends off (except gas stations and some stores within a certain distance from sea ports) and get to spend time with their families rather than with shopping. And teenagers don't get to hangout in the malls the whole weekend either.

My friends took me to a Chinese buffet restaurant in town. The food was actually quite good. The workers were all Chinese and our waiter came from Guangzhou (Canton) and has been living in Denmark for 6 years. She told me that the owner of the restaurant came from Hong Kong. We had a little chat in Cantonese. And I was left puzzled as to how a young woman from Guangzhou ended up living in Scandinavia. And to think the poor woman has to learn those unpronounceable Danish vowels and consonants.

After shopping, we stopped by Soren and Marguerite's home (their 2nd son and his wife) for tea before heading back to Grenaa. Their nine year-old daughter baked the dessert and their teenage son served the tea, coffee and hot chocolate. The Danes are taught to be independent at an early age.

Short Days

This is the first time I was in Denmark at this time of the year. The days are very short. Sunrise happens after 8am and sunset starts at about 4pm. As a night-owl, I actually quite enjoy such short days. I always find myself much more productive after dark. In 2000, I went to Denmark in July, when the sun rose at 4am and set at about 10pm. One can really feel the seasons when one lives so far away from the equator.

To create a warm ambience, candles are used generously for meals and tea. It really warms up a cold winter and creates a beautiful setting for conversation.

11. Dallas For A Party

November 29, 2004 - Dallas, Texas, USA

Homeless In Dallas

I went back to Dallas for a short break between Europe and Central America. The break was necessary for me to change from winter clothes to summer clothes. When the plane landed in Dallas, it felt very strange when I realized that I no longer had a home in this city where I had lived for more than 13 years. For a short moment I was disoriented and unsure of what I was doing.

Well, I was only in Dallas for 3 days and did only a handful of things. I ate in my favorite Chinese restaurant - Jade Garden - twice. I went to church. And I shopped for a replacement digital camera. Speaking of which, if you are in the market for a digital camera, I suggest that you take a close look at Canon. I used to own a different brand but chose Canon this time, mainly for its ease of use. And I have been a very satisfied customer so far.

Birthday Party

My friends, Mike & Bob, who let me stay in their "guest wing" for the weekend, also threw a party for me. Quite a few of my friends showed up even though it was the Saturday after Thanksgiving. When I read the birthday cards, most of which had the numbers 40 printed on them, the fact that I was turning 40 sank in. The truth is that I don't feel old and I don't mind getting old. In fact, I will take "getting older" over "the alternative" any day. Inside, I feel that I haven't changed since the late 20s. And now I have a whole year to do young and somewhat less responsible things!

The Best Birthday Gift Day

A friend of mine, Neal, collected messages from my friends across the country and the world who couldn't be present at the party. Their messages were read by the friends at the party. I was really touched as the messages were being read. Very kind words were said and I was reminded once more how blessed I am for having so many good friends sprinkled across the globe. It was the best birthday gift I have ever received, thanks to Neal again.

Heading For The Unknown - Central America

On November 29th, I flew down to San Jose, Costa Rica, to start the Latin American part of the sabbatical. My timing for the sabbatical was very much determined by the end date of my last project. It ended up I would arrive in Central America when schools were getting ready for their month long Christmas break. At any rate, I had to follow the plan and see what lied ahead. I do have a place to stay, and quite a few friends to help me. Other than that, nothing is definite. It will be a real test of my adventurous spirit.

12. Hola! Welcome To Costa Rica

December 15, 2004 - San Jose, Costa Rica

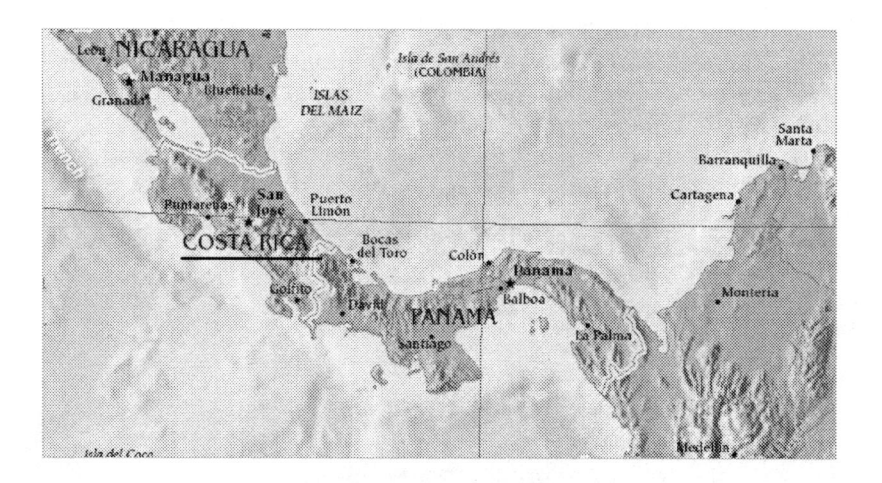

Started The Latin American Portion Of The Sabbatical

Before I started writing about this leg of the sabbatical, I wondered that I might not have much of interest to write about. I have been to Costa Rica 8 or 9 times in the last 5 years and things are starting to get too familiar to catch my attention. The last two weeks proved me wrong - I have jotted down plenty of topics. I will keep this one somewhat brief, if I can help it, or I won't be able to publish it before leaving for Panama on December 17.

I Arrived Feeling Uneasy

It's been two weeks since I took that flight from Dallas to San Jose, Costa Rica. I was sitting next to a gringo artist who had been living in the rainforest here for the last 10 years. I was in 9B on an American Airlines Boeing 757 - exit row bulkhead, the best seat in economy class. If you are an AA frequent flier junkie, you can visualize exactly what I am talking about. For some strange reasons, I meet the most interesting people in this very seat. Another example: when I went to Dominican Republic last year, I talked to this gentleman for 8 hours and our topics of conversation could be material for a few books. We talked about everything from work, to raising children, the economy, religion, life and death, our innermost fears, what make us tick and the purpose of our lives. I did not know his name until, during the layover in Miami, one of my friends came up and asked me to introduce them. She thought we had known each other for years. That's when we got each other's name and five hours had already passed since we started talking when boarding just started back in Dallas. Now, please don't get the idea that I always talk to strangers like this. It really doesn't happen so often as you may think.

On this flight two weeks ago, this gentleman told me he was mugged at dusk near downtown this time of the year two years ago. They cleared him out. He warned me because I look like a foreigner and an easy target. Where he was mugged is very close to where I take the bus to where I live. So, I was quite alarmed the first week. Before leaving Dallas, I had left my gold chain and swapped my Skaagen watch for a Timex. Now when I go out, I leave all my credit cards and ATM card at home. My wallet is THIN - it contains only a copy of my passport and cash! I only go out with the cards when I know I need them. My Costa Rican family warns me of the same. Personally, I never feel that unsafe here. But one should almost always heed the advice of the locals when traveling abroad.

Let The Cash Flow!

The workers receive an extra paycheck, known as aguinado, at the beginning of December. I learned, technically, you get your average monthly salary over a 12 month period ending in October of the current year. How's that for precise information? And they are all out shopping for Christmas. This year, I have witnessed 4 countries shopping frantically for Christmas. The lesson? No matter what language they speak and what the temperature is outside, it's crazy all the same. Oh, I shall witness a 5th one when I get to Panama. Fun, fun, fun.

Avenida Central is packed with shoppers all day long. Also conspicuous is the presence of the police force. They are everywhere. They even built a few little platforms - as if they were lifeguards on the beach - to afford the officers on duty a better view of the crowds. This indicates to me that pick pocketing must be really serious at this time. Everybody needs some extra cash for the holidays - the charity organizations, the poor, and the thieves. Everybody is collecting money for something.

To fend them off, I resorted to lying a few times by saying in broken Spanish with poor conjugation that I don't speak Spanish, so stop explaining to me why you want my money already. I am unemployed, darn it! Then this little guy came out of nowhere asking me in English – "Do you speak English?" I gave him my best confused 'huh?' expression and kept walking, pretending I don't even recognize the language. Good thing nobody came after me speaking Chinese!

In Search Of Volunteer Work

Well, I spent the first two weeks making contacts and such. I had an interview with the State orphanage last Tuesday. They want me to teach English and computers to teenage boys and girls (14-18) when school resumes in February. I read from their website that while most of these kids are basically good kids, some of them are drug addicts or (ex) sex workers, and they already have had a tough life at such a young age. The orphanage said they would call me in January, and somehow I feel that I shouldn't put all my eggs in one basket.

Then came a classic networking story. I went to visit my Spanish teacher. She and I became friends after meeting each other in 2000. Over the years, I have met her husband and their three children. Here's the power of networking: My teacher's husband's cousin's husband is the man who is in charge of a church community - not a Catholic one, obviously. My teacher set up an interview with the pastor for me. It happened this morning. We had a great chat. They wanted me to start tomorrow to help with a Christmas Pageant, building sets and sorting out the donated Christmas presents for the poor kids in the neighborhood. I had to defer working with them until January because of the planned trip. They are just as happy to wait until January.

This week I have been helping a school proofreading and translating their website into English. It's been a fun job, even though no students are around this time of the year.

Why Panama For Christmas?

Well, my Costa Rican family informed me that they had already made plans to go there for 10 days when I first arrived. And they wanted me to join them. I told them it would depend on what happens with these interviews. Not much happened during the first week. When I came home from the interview last week, I was convinced that nothing could happen until January.

More importantly, while I enjoy being alone, I really don't want to be left alone here and be solely responsible for the house for 10 days. It's a big responsibility. I really don't know how some of the basic things work. If anything should go wrong, I don't think I can properly explain to the 911 operator what the problem is. Also, the household appliances work a little differently. For example, if I am not careful with the washing machine, I can accidentally flood the house. In fact, it's so complicated that I simply do not bother to learn to operate it anymore. You have to baby sit it during the rinse cycle or the flood will happen. I just let them do the wash and I do all the ironing - one of my favorite therapeutic activities. Too bad they don't show Golden Girls here. Otherwise, ironing while watching my Golden Girls speaking Spanish will really make my day!

When I considered all these concerns, I realized it's actually a really good idea to go to Panama with them. Merry Christmas!

13. Panama For Christmas Part I

December 26, 2004 - Panama City, Panama

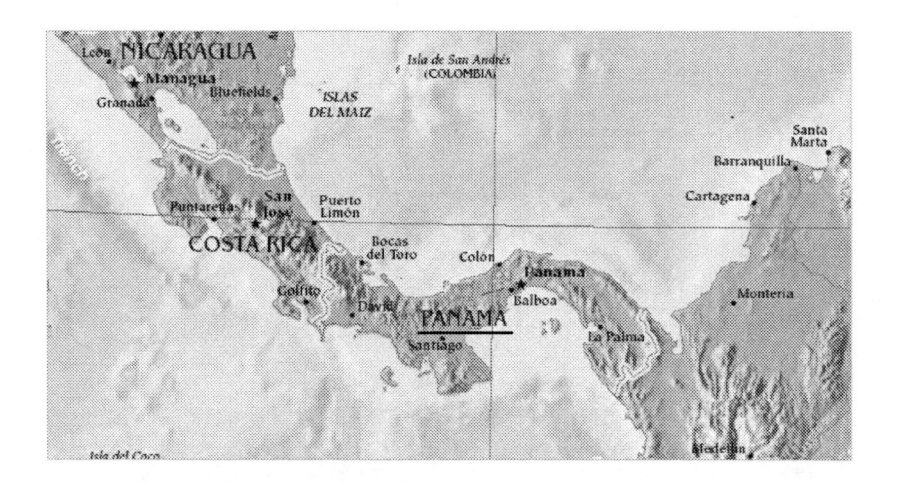

The 17-Hour Bus Ride (That Ended Up Taking 28 Hours)

Four of us, Alvaro, Gilberto, Claudina (Gilberto's mom) and I, set out for Panama City on December 17. We chose to go by bus (for $50 per person round trip) instead of by air (for $200 PP RT). I am becoming a good tico! (Tico - what a native Costa Rican calls himself.) It was supposed to be a 17-hour ride, leaving San Jose at 1pm and arriving in Panama City at 6am the next morning.

We made our first stop at 6:30 for dinner. The same driver had been driving the bus for 5.5 hours. Right before we pulled into the restaurant, there was a minor explosion under the bus and we thought it blew a tire. We ate and the driver took the bus to the gas station to have it fixed. Meanwhile, I was wondering if he would be the sole driver throughout the night all the way to Panama City. That's a scary thought. I never did find out.

An hour later, we continued on the Pan American highway and headed south. Shortly after nine, in the middle of the jungle, the bus broke down. After standing on the highway with our luggage for two hours, in the middle of absolutely nowhere, we were picked up by another bus from that same company - Panaline. That's when we realized that the border closed at 10pm. We were to spend the night on the bus at the border. Fortunately, my ability to sleep anywhere anytime gave me much rest throughout the night as well as much of the trip during the day. My fellow bus riders were kept awake from the discomfort and by a woman who snored like a freight train. I didn't hear a thing!

Crossing the border between Costa Rica and Panama was the most confusing thing I have ever experienced. We started to line up on the Costa Rican side at 5am – it didn't open until 6am, but a line formed shortly before 5am and nobody wanted to miss out, human nature is similar everywhere – and eventually left Panama border control after 8am, after joining multiple lines on both sides of the border.

We finally got to Panama City at 5pm, 28 hours after the trip started. The driver who picked us up on the highway the night before drove all the way. It was a good thing that I slept more than 18 hours of the trip. The trip included some very tricky twists and turns high up in the mountain and I hate to think at which one the driver might have chosen to dose off from fatigue.

The bus went through a bad part of town after crossing the Bridge of the Americas. My first impression of Panama City wasn't so good. For a country that owns one of the most important water passages in the world, I was surprised that the average person was not financially better off than what met the eyes. The apartment buildings were run down. It also felt very dangerous. When my friends asked the accused snoring woman if we were in Panama City, I had the awkward awakening that they had never been there before. And all along I had the impression that they knew the city really well - they didn't read any guide books about Panama and didn't bring a map. That was also the moment I started to pay attention to everything.

From The West Coast To The East Coast In Less Than 90 Minutes

Our hotel was in Colon, on the Atlantic end of the Panama Canal, which was clear across the continent from where we were. A taxi took us to Avis in town where we picked up our prearranged rental car. Since the car was in my name and I was the one most awake, for obvious reasons, I had the honor of doing one of the craziest things in my life - driving in Latin America. The map given by Avis was more like a sketch. In the city, only the main thoroughfares were named. They only drew lines in the subdivision and didn't bother to name them, and that's also where the rental place was. It was most useless. Nevertheless, we found our way to the highway and got to the Atlantic side in less than 90 minutes. A small Christmas miracle in my book.

On the road, I realized something very strange. Even though I was driving from the Pacific coast to the Atlantic coast, I was actually heading north-northwest the whole time. Did you know that the Atlantic side of the Panama Canal actually lies further west of the Pacific side of the canal? Interesting, eh?

Currency

The official currency of Panama is Balboa, symbol "B./". The government issues coins. When it comes to notes, they use US dollars ONLY, making it US$1 equivalent to B./1. The coins are the exact denominations and sizes of US coins, but they have slightly different names. Well, they are in Spanish:

Medio Balboa (half dollar)
Cuarto de Balboa (a quarter)
Decimo de Balboa (a dime)
Cinco Centesimos de Balboa (a nickel)
Un Centesimo de Balboa (a penny)

The guide books say that there are coins of One Balboa, but I didn't see any. The official Panama guide book also says that adopting the US currency is the most important financial asset for the country, arguably more so than the Canal.

I don't have any problem with them using US notes as their official currency. What I don't understand is why they insist on calling it a different name. In the stores, they mostly use the symbol "B./", but the $ sign is occasionally seen. In the foreign exchange market, one dollar is equal to slightly less than one balboa. What exactly does that mean? I am puzzled.

The City Of Colon

Colon is the second largest city of Panama. Panama is very proud that Colon is also home to the world's second largest free trade zone featuring more than 1,000 stores, after Hong Kong, where the whole city is one big free trade zone. Should you wonder why I was not exactly impressed by their "Zona Libre" in Colon?

The population of Colon (and of Panama on the whole) tells the story of the construction of the Panama Canal. Many Africans were brought in from the Caribbean islands during the project and they stayed on to create their families. Blacks, hence, made up a large percentage of the population there. There is also a very conspicuous amount of Chinese people - running a number of Chinese restaurants, laundromats, grocery stores and such.

My impression is that the people here are not a very happy bunch. I was shouted at with a "Qué?" in a fast food joint when the woman behind the counter could not hear me. This kind of customer service was rather commonplace. Rarely did we hear "thank you" when we paid for our purchases. Whenever the people showed any sign of customer service and smiled (it happened a few times), we felt really surprised and honored. And we always commented on it afterwards. I wondered what made these individuals different from the larger society they found themselves in.

The city is very run down, with the exception of the Passenger Cruise Port. On the streets, the people walked at an uncanny uniform speed, which vividly reminded me of the movie Zombie. And they don't smile. Often times there was little emotion on their faces. And they crossed the street when they reached the curb; seemingly the vehicular traffic had no impact on them. To be fair, I probably didn't look much better myself as part of my digestion system left me and went on vacation of its own. I couldn't imagine everyone in town had my problem though.

We went to do laundry on Christmas Eve, in a laundromat run by a Chinese family, of course. I saw that the Chinese people have the same kind of customer service. It must be in the water. Granted, they were quite nice to me, given that I was a fresh Chinese face in town. I struck up a conversation with a local woman (a big one) at the laundromat and we had an interesting and nice chat. She was watching out for me. The laundromat is actually a great place to meet the locals.

14. Panama For Christmas Part II

December 29, 2004 - David, Panama

Portobelo

We drove down to Portobelo, a small town on the Caribbean, leading to the Isla Grande beach. It was a beautiful drive and it was also my favorite day of the trip. We met a few happy salespersons and we were very much left alone. Nobody begged and no one looked at us as if we were some sort of prey.

Panama City

We drove back and forth to Panama City a few times to see the Canal and mostly for my friends to go shopping. The malls here are of very high quality and they can fit in any city in North America, which also means that they are boring for some. Here I witnessed my 5th country doing Christmas shopping this season. I don't know where the people get their money to do all this shopping. There were long lines at the cashiers everywhere we went. My Costa Rican friends said that the "credit card phenomenon" had reached Central America and everyone is borrowing from their future.

We left Colon for good on Christmas Day and moved to Panama City for two days to do some city sightseeing. The shops were closed but the grocery stores were all open, to my big surprise. They are considered essential service, like gas stations, so they stay open almost all year long. I learned that they only close one day of the year - Good Friday.

We drove around town and found the rich part of Panama city on the Pacific coast. It is incredible how many luxurious apartment buildings are under construction. We heard from a taxi driver later on that those are mostly bought by foreigners from Colombia, Venezuela, the US, and the Chinese. Again, draw your own conclusions as I am not offering any.

I saw on the news the next day the great tsunami tragedy in Southeast Asia. I was glued to the Spanish CNN for a few hours and tried to understand the magnitude of the disaster. My friends were not in the mood to discuss it. But what can one say about it really? While we do what we can financially for these disaster-stricken fellow human beings, we should also learn that we really must not take life for granted. It's a gift that can be taken away or interrupted at any given moment, regardless of where you find yourself.

David

To break the long road trip into two pieces, we spent two days in David, a city about an hour and half away from the Costa Rican border. It was a beautiful 5-hour bus ride from Panama City to David. We have a friend who lives there. The people in David display a personality trait that is more commonly found in Costa Rica than in Panama, so it was a very refreshing change. It's a very small town but we had a good visit with Leslie and her family. Leslie studied medicine in Costa Rica and returned to Panama to practice; she now works for a government hospital.

New Year Eve In Costa Rica

We were back to Costa Rica late on the 29th. Many shops here in Costa Rica are closed after Christmas and would not open again until after New Year's Day - my kind of holiday attitude. Even the government offices were mostly shut down and it was practically impossible to get any serious business done in this period.

We were invited to a New Year's Eve party (barbecue) at a friend's house. Her daughters and sons-in-law and grandchildren were all there. Firework and fire crackers broke out at midnight. They were enjoying it much more than I was. It was not comforting to know that these people are shooting fireworks in heavily populated areas. My only consolation was that one of the sons-in-law is a fireman and he was listening to a walkie-talkie type radio all night long, in case big problems arose and he had to report to duty.

15. First Trip Of 2005 - Puerto Viejo

January 9, 2005 - San Jose, Costa Rica

I Just Can't Say NO

I am almost ashamed to write this entry - it really sounds like excessive traveling. But then, I think I already crossed that line when I started this sabbatical. Well, here it goes.

At the same time I accepted the invitation from my Costa Rican family to go to Panama (before anything could be confirmed with the charity organizations), I got an e-mail from Reid, a friend I met in the language school in Guanajuato, Mexico, in early 2002. I use the word "friend" more loosely, and more sincerely, than most people I know.

Reid read my Newsletter and informed me that he was coming to Costa Rica for a few days with his mother and wondered if I could join or visit them at the Caribbean coast. I really didn't know Reid very well, though I remembered that I enjoyed hanging out with him and a few others in Mexico. He's an attorney (so he has a certain level of intelligence for interesting and thoughtful conversations), yet he is not at all obnoxious as one might expect from an attorney. Moreover, I have been to this country 9 times and I have only seen the Pacific coast once, and have never been to the Caribbean coast. I kept telling myself that I would wait to see these "tourist" places when my American friends come to visit me. So, this trip meets all the conditions.

By the way, I have not seen the cloud forest, volcanoes, the Pacific Northwest and many other wonderful sights here yet. If any of you is interested, come on down and I will be happy to take a few days off to see them with you - free translation service offered, if necessary.

Hooking Up

I met them at the airport on Tuesday the 4th and we headed out to Limon, the biggest Costa Rican city on the Atlantic. It's actually very small, mostly black and Chinese, just like Colon in Panama, but the people are much more cheerful. Reid's mom, in her sixties, has more energy than both Reid and I do, combined. She still runs the marathon frequently. It was her first visit south of the border and she enjoyed it tremendously, mostly owing to her own generous spirit, kindness, sense of curiosity, and energy; and the company helped a little! We hit it off right at the start when we watched Jeopardy at the hotel before dinner. The three of us combined could have won some money from the show if they would have allowed us to participate as a team!

Puerto Viejo

We spent the night in Limon and headed down the coast to Puerto Viejo by bus, a 90-minute ride along the beautiful Caribbean. It's a small and peaceful town of nine square blocks. The people are very friendly and there is a surprisingly large variety of wonderful restaurants. We found a Thai restaurant and it was so good that we ate there 3 times.

Some of the beaches here are covered with black sand. We had fun taking long walks along the beaches, eating and drinking the freshest of food, biking, bird-watching, and talking to the locals and travelers alike. A great time was had by all three rather experienced travelers.

The flowers and plants are plentiful and beautiful. I wished that Tom, my gardener friend, were there to help us understand what we were looking at. There were also many birds. It is a paradise tucked away. There were a lot of North Americans and Europeans visiting this time of the year, almost too many. You wouldn't think so many people would be taking vacations the first week of the New Year, would you? I suppose many students are taking advantage of the holiday before school starts again.

There was a Surf Competition for the weekend; the prize: US$5,000! You can live in this town for a year with that much money. Many gringos and Europeans are in the competition. The three of us hoped that a local boy would win, but we couldn't stay to watch the competition as Ann and Reid had an early flight bound for Kansas on Saturday.

We Met The Ultimate Brave Souls

While we strolled through town, we found a new restaurant/bakery getting ready for its grand opening on the weekend. We talked to the owners (a young couple in their 20s) for a little and learned of their adventurous story. This Minnesotan couple came to Puerto Viejo to visit a year ago and decided to move down here. They went home and started the plan to open a restaurant here (he's the baker). They bought an old school bus from Gypsies in Minnesota and converted it into a vehicle suitable for long distance traveling - put in solar energy panels, kitchens, bathrooms, etc. They bought cooking equipment and utensils for the restaurant. Then they drove this old school bus all the way from Minnesota to Costa Rica - crossing at least 6 borders. They are just learning Spanish now and I wondered how they explained all the things that were on the bus to the border patrol officers, let alone the bus itself!

Well, the bus broke down in Mexico and the brakes went out in the mountains of Honduras. They managed to communicate with the locals to have it fixed; and they finally got to Puerto Viejo two and half months ago, rented an empty restaurant, renovated it, furnished it, secured perishable supplies for the kitchen, and are now posed for the grand opening during the weekend's surf competition. They plan to live upstairs of the restaurant when it's ready; meanwhile, they have been living in the bus since they left Minnesota more than 3 months ago. To add to the challenge, they are now expecting their first baby in April. We wished them the best. Love truly can overcome any obstacles.

Back To Reality (If You Can Call My Life Here Real)

Well, I will start teaching English next week. My initial assignment will be for a month, 2 hours a day, 2 days a week. Meanwhile, I need to finish up the translation job that I did in December for a school. And I will let you know as things develop.

16. Reality As I Know It

January 14 , 2005 – San Jose, Costa Rica

Disastrous Flooding Over The Weekend

With the recent enormous number of disasters happening in the world–the aftermath of the tsunami in Asia, the mudslide in southern California, the flooding in the southwestern states, the record-breaking cold weather in the north, not to mention the distant yet endless war in Iraq (does anyone remember why we went there to start with?)—I don't suppose you are aware of the flooding disaster that hit Costa Rica last weekend.

It rained incessantly in some areas for two days starting Saturday and the destruction has been awful. It rained in the central valley where the capital San Jose is, but it let up after a few hours. Some of the most affected areas are in the cities up north and the remote villages in Limon province on the Caribbean. To date, more than 6,000 have lost their homes and I could not find the number of deaths and missing. On the TV I have seen people swimming on the streets. Considering the recent worldwide disasters, 6,000 does not sound like a large number. Nevertheless, that is still 6,000 too many. Besides, this is a small country of 4 million people, so percentage-wise it is significant. And the infrastructure damage is numerous. Consequently, the local TV stations are doing fundraising shows and the tsunami in Asia no longer occupies the front page of the local papers.

It is summer here now, and it's supposed to be the dry season until May, yet it has been raining much more than usual. The most affected province, Limon, is where Reid, Ann and I spent last week. We left the area Friday, spared from the flood by just one day.

The Church Where I Work

Well, it is high time I talked about my work here, supposedly the core of my sabbatical. This week, I started working for a church organization: Comunidad Cristiana - Vida Abundante (Christian

Community - Abundant Life). The church is less than 5 miles away from the house, but it takes an hour by bus, with a change of bus in the city of Guadalupe, costing a total of 70 cents. It would take 10 minutes by taxi, at about $3.5. I take the bus.

Here in Costa Rica we are relatively close to the equator (N09°57.318' W084°0.165' to be exact) and the blazing sun prevents walking this distance. In fact, I have already become quite tan over the last month and look more Filipino than Chinese at this point.

To the surprise of many, Vida Abundante is NOT a Catholic church, but an evangelical one. In spite of my Catholic background, it does not matter to me the least bit as I am not very "religious," even though I do claim to be a Christian. For me, religion is a very private matter and I am not good at, nor am I interested in, talking about it. That is not to say I do not have any opinion on religion, if you must ask. I firmly believe that religion should be lived, not talked about, that's all.

I am the first to admit that reading people is not my forte. Having said that, I think the people in this place seem very nice. Well, they have been very nice to me so far. The church also runs a bilingual elementary school next to the church building – rather, the church bungalow. It serves an estimated 4,000 members with 4 services each week: one on Saturday evening, two on Sunday morning, and one on Sunday evening. The pastor told me that all four services are identical, including the jokes and music. This is done on purpose so that people are not tempted to come to more than one service on any given weekend.

The church runs more than 35 social programs for its members and the community around it. For instance, it has an open education program for anyone who did not finish high school to work towards the secondary education certificate - the students range from poor teenagers (immigrants from Nicaragua and the indigenous people) to the elderly. It also holds support group meetings for drug and alcohol addicts - confidentially, of course. It even has a support group for teenage moms. It also works closely with the local orphanages. You can imagine this is a fairly open-minded place. Well, I will let you know if and when my opinion should change.

My First Assignment

When I visualized the sabbatical in the last three years, for the longest time I thought I would be doing some teaching and lots of manual labor such as painting the buildings, cleaning the ground, and so on. When I met with the pastor in charge of administration at the beginning of the week, he told me about this computer project that he is leading (IT is not his background) and he wanted me to be a part of it. I accepted with much reservation. It's a networking and hardware project in the first phase, far from my expertise and cup of tea. I haven't messed with computer networks since I left the auto-parts manufacturer in 1995. That's about 200 years ago in computer years!

That same morning, 30 minutes after arriving at the church and accepting the assignment, the pastor took me to my first meeting away from the church to talk to a local volunteer about the network design. It was in Spanish. It was tech-talk. Those are TWO foreign languages! Obviously I didn't say much, but they didn't completely lose me either, and I survived. Much to my surprise.

One day while I was walking between the buildings, watching the people cleaning the ground in preparation for the weekend's service, it dawned on me that manual labor is cheap and abundant here; of course they would want to use me in a very different capacity. And my computer background is what they can use the most at the moment. With this realization, I look at the job with a very different attitude and vow to do my best to help them, in their own terms and at their pace. Lesson number two of the sabbatical: unconditional gift. I am looking to my buddies at my company for technical advice. They have been very responsive so far and I am most grateful.

Le Presento Señor Pang - Profesor De Inglés

Meanwhile, I am teaching two teenagers English twice a week. This should only last until early February as the new school year will begin then. They are a lot of fun and teach me a lot about the culture from their point of view. Incidentally, I teach them in a city called Tres Rios, an hour and half from the church by bus. And it is two hours from the house, which means that I spend almost five hours traveling from one place to another on Tuesdays and Thursdays. Someone recommended a scooter, but I am not sure.

One of the pastors asked me if I could give him lessons and he was willing to pay. I accepted him as a student but turned him down for his offer of money, giving him the reason that since he is part of the church, I did not feel right charging him. Realistically, how many dollars an hour can I charge a pastor? More importantly, I really do not have the time to do detailed lesson plans for hours at a time; the pain in London is still too fresh. Accepting money will imply a much higher level of commitment, not that mine is low, to be sure!

I shared with him that people tend not to take things too seriously if they are free. And I told him that our agreement will end should this happen. Since I am free, I have the luxury of choosing to teach only those who truly want to learn. He concurred. Ticos mostly learn American English in school. I also warned him that he may have a weird mix of American/British/Chinese/Spanish accent as a result of studying with me for a few months. It didn't deter him. My first lessons with both groups have been most enjoyable for all. They will be back. So will I.

17. At Home In Costa Rica I

January 28, 2005 - San Jose, Costa Rica

Routine, But Far From Boredom

Tico or Tica - n. nickname for someone born in Costa Rica, for male and female respectively, adj. related to ticos

It just occurred to me that I have not written about my accommodations here in Costa Rica. Well, the truth is that someone asked me about this by e-mail and it was an unintended negligence on my part.

Life is getting into a routine cycle here: three days in the church, two days teaching at the language school, and then sick on the weekends. It was becoming somewhat predictable and, understandably, I am slowly losing my sensitivity to the environment. For one, I know I do not turn my head nearly as much anymore. However, to "protect" myself, I still have to consciously "fake" boredom in the buses that are full so that the people do not think I am a recently arrived tourist, i.e. easy target.

There are in fact lots of Chinese living in Costa Rica, more than 100,000 – which is not unlikely at all, as I was told – but I could not confirm that figure. Somehow my friends are convinced that I won't be able to fit in as a Tico Chinese, even with my mouth shut, which makes me an easy target for the potential criminals. Incidentally, when I am in public and dealing with strangers (this was an everyday event for me in Panama), it's not uncommon at all for people to address me as "chino" - literally "Chinese Man" or "Chinaman." I thought it was rather amusing that the people use it to my face. When I told my tico family about this, they said this is how they address the local Chinese as well, and they wondered if I was offended. Heck no, dangling phrases are offensive to me, but not a little word like "chino." I am sure if I were born here, I wouldn't find it quite amusing. Imagine a Latino walking into a MacDonald's in the US and the uniformed guy behind the counter saying, "Hello Mexican, what would you like?" That's how it feels.

Seriously, I am much more amused than offended in my case. How did I get from the subtitle "Routine" to Mexican?

The House And The Apartment

I live in a 3 bedroom, 2.5 bath apartment, with Alvaro and Gilberto, and Gilberto's mom, Doña Claudina. Alvaro's sister Vivian, her husband Rodrigo and their (very cute) 7 month-old son Felipe live in the 2 bedroom, 1.5 bath house next door. The apartment and the house are connected through the garden. Alvaro and Gilberto own the whole property.

I met Alvaro and Gilberto through my first language school in San Jose when I came to study Spanish in 1999 and the school placed me in their family. We have since become friends over the years. When I told them of my sabbatical plan last year, they offered me their spare bedroom. That's how I ended up having my own bedroom in Costa Rica. The bedroom has a small modern sofa/bed for one person, suitable for someone who doesn't toss and turn too much, or he will find himself on the floor in the middle of the night. Since I am living out of one big and one small suitcase, that room is plenty big for me.

When Doña Claudina moved in with them in November (a surprise to all concerned), a week or so before my arrival, the house lost a suite to the apartment to accommodate her. Alvaro is an architect and surveyor, so he masterminded the modification project. Even though the apartment has more rooms, the house is still significantly larger than the apartment. For instance, in the apartment, it is technically impossible to separate the living room from the dining room, and the dining room from the kitchen. And if you try, you can have one foot in the living room and one foot in the kitchen, with the dining room between them.

Due to the limit on space, our dining table is a retrofitted sewing machine top, measuring no more than 20" x 30." That also happens to be the only table we have. We usually have brunches in the apartment on the weekends, all 7 of us. It works. Considering I once lived in an apartment of 400 sq. ft. in Hong Kong and there were 17 of us at the peak time, this apartment in Costa Rica is downright spacious. By the way, it is very popular to convert these old sewing machines into tables. There is a chain restaurant in town called Spoon that uses this type of table exclusively. Of course, their tables are considerably larger than the one in our apartment.

Another not so funny note: there is a small sitting area upstairs, next to the phone. That's where I do all my typing using my laptop. The laptop literally sits on top of my lap every time I use the computer. My neck suffers a lot as a result.

Security, The Costa Rican Style

The house is located half way up the mountain, about 6-7 miles from downtown San Jose, making it breezy in the daytime and quite cold at night. It is situated behind a 24-hour guarded gate, along with 30 or so families. However, this still is not sufficient security for most and some families install garage doors for their already secured car ports. This happened in our house last Christmas. From the outside, nobody can see anything inside the house at the ground level. The reverse is also true, unfortunately. All one can see while inside the house are walls, and the sunlight is mostly blocked.

All the homes are "designed" to prevent people from breaking in. For more than 99% of the houses I have seen, all windows at the ground level are reinforced with iron bars to deter breaking in. In addition, there are normally multiple locks on the front doors. It requires keys to open them, even from inside. The carport is, of course, protected by another layer of iron bars, also under locks. While these security measures lock out the would-be criminals, they also effectively LOCK the residents IN.

If you have traveled with me, you know I can sleep anywhere anytime, and deep is my sleep. If a fire should break out during the night, I would be fried. There's no doubt about it. When I sleep, I keep my keys right next to my bed, in case of an evacuation. There is certainly a market in this country for locks that can be opened from the inside without keys. As far as I am concerned, when a security measure becomes a threat itself, it's gone too far.

18. Moving About In Greater San Jose

February 5, 2005 - San Jose, Costa Rica

I like Costa Rica, but I like it for reasons very different from why I like Denmark. Costa Rica is full of friendly people and it is a beautiful and eco-diverse country; there is no denying that. However, I like Costa Rica mostly because it brings back memories of my childhood. I suppose it sounds strange to find childhood memories all the way across the globe. The transportation system is one of the things that bring me, emotionally, back to Hong Kong in the early 70s.

Taking The Buses

I use the buses a lot, up to 6 times a day on Tuesdays and Thursdays. What I like about taking the bus is that it offers me a chance to observe the locals in a natural setting, up close. It isn't uncommon at all to see men and younger people ceding their seats to the elderly, mothers with young children and pregnant women. But, taking the bus itself is not an easy task if you don't live here, if you can't read and don't speak a little Spanish.

I can't even start to guess how many different bus companies there are that serve the Greater San Jose area. From what I can see, all the buses go downtown from the suburbs, and each suburb (or the general area in that direction) is served by a different bus company. Since San Jose is in the central valley, practically all the buses go from downtown to the mountains surrounding the valley.

To complicate matters, there are no bus numbers on the buses, even though some companies put route numbers at their bus stops. On the windshield, the buses have a number of bumper-sticker-like signs that show their destinations and the major landmarks they travel by. The landmarks usually include a mall, a university, a cinema, a major grocery store, etc. To know which bus to take, one must know exactly where one is heading - all the buses that head to the same general direction look alike and show similar destinations, with one or two keyword differences. I have taken the wrong bus before.

The buses are not air-conditioned and, in the city, all of them are single deck and most of them have hard seats. Almost all the buses have front and rear doors. The bus driver is also in charge of collecting the fare and making changes. I think the drivers drive the same bus everyday since the areas surrounding the driver's seat are highly personalized. Some put religious items, while others put personalized signs to advise the passengers to pay when they board or not to rush the driver to go faster, continuing to tell the passengers to leave the house earlier the next morning if they find themselves being late for wherever they are going. These are always great fun to read.

To keep the drivers honest, the bus companies install electronic counters on both doors. Passengers are not supposed to board the bus from the back. The counters are two metal bars, and they count the number of people going through those bars. Most foreigners, myself included, often get yelled at by the bus drivers because we tend to stand between those bars while we wait for the change. Sometimes there are people riding on the steps (friends, family and other company employees) so that they don't have to pay. The rule is that once they cross the electronic counter, they must pay.

Most drivers tend to drive with both doors left open. It's great for ventilation, and it allows people to get off the bus whenever the bus stops, no matter whether it's at a designated bus stop or not. This is especially handy at rush hour. Again, my home is less than 7 miles from downtown, and the journey takes a good hour during peak hours. In other words, the average speed is less than 7mph! It takes about 45 minutes at other times.

At the bus terminal or along the route, people board the buses and sell small items like snacks, ball-point pens (this happens often), key chains, or flash lights. They sometimes do fundraising or begging, and one time this guy came on board and sold language pamphlets, while promoting his language teaching services.

Taking The Taxis

While my tico family tends to disagree with me on this one, I find the taxis very cheap here. For example, I can go to Tres Rios (where I teach on Tue & Thu afternoons) by taxi for about $4-5 and the journey takes about 20-25 minutes. The same journey by bus takes almost two hours at rush hour, for about 75 cents. Taxis are metered and they are plentiful. However, that doesn't mean anyone can take the taxi "successfully." To make my point, first I will have to talk about the address system – or the lack of it, rather.

Here's what an address of a friend of mine looks like (with the numbers changed to protect the innocent), translated into English:

From the Shell Gas Station in La Uruca
200 meters north, 100 meters east,
50 meters north, 100 meters west,
Carranza Sub Division
White House, Black Fence, On High
San Jose, Costa Rica

Once, this friend told me that his father painted the exterior of the house. I asked him what color he painted it, just in case I needed to update my address book accordingly!

When I write to this friend, I actually put ALL this information on the envelope. Streets in Costa Rica are not traditionally named. The Spanish word for address is "dirección," and here in Costa Rica, it's literally the direction. When you ask where something is, people always start with a landmark, the Shell Gas Station in this case, and direct you from there. Note that it is possible that the 100 meters in the address above MAY be longer than the 200 meters. Basically, one block equals 100 meters, regardless of its actual length. Ergo, around half way up the block is 50 meters. If it leans towards one end, then it's 25 or 75 meters. To make things worse, sometimes the landmark used is "the old something something", i.e., it no longer exists and something else is on the site, but the old thing was so prominent that everybody is supposed to know where it was.

Granted, the city started a project to name the streets years ago. It actually numbered some of the streets and avenues around downtown and put up signs at selected corners. But nobody uses them. The only street that people know by heart is Central Avenue, but it's because it's central (the location/direction), not because it says so on the map. The city is now engaged in giving numbers to the houses, so that a change in paint color does not entail a change of address.

This presents a problem when you take a taxi. Unless you are going to a hotel, a restaurant, a church, or something that is a landmark itself, you will need to be a back seat driver to direct the taxi driver to your destination. You start by giving the landmark. When you get to the landmark, you tell the driver when and where to turn left or right until you get to your destination. If you don't know how to get there, the driver doesn't mind as the meter keeps ticking until he finds it. In other words, taking a taxi requires some prior visual knowledge of the destination and some Spanish skills (turning left, right, go straight, etc.) Remember, you can't really look things up in a map. What map? Nobody has a map in the car. The only maps that I have seen are the tourist maps for the downtown area.

Another unusual thing about taking the taxi is that male passengers sit in the front, even if one travels alone. It was very awkward for me at the beginning, but then I realized that sitting in the back probably screams to the driver that I am new here, so go ahead and take me the long route or rob me blind. I have since learned to sit in the front. However, if you are a woman traveling alone, regardless of whether you are a foreigner or a local, you should never sit in the front, because doing so signals a very distinct message to the driver.

Every morning I leave the house, Doña Claudina tells me in Spanish "May God accompany you!" I always reply with a "Thank you. See you later." However, in my mind, I usually think that with so much aggressing driving here, God had better accompany me, or He WILL see me in person very soon. And I pray a lot on the road. Taking the taxi can sometimes mean taking your life in your hands. Some of the taxi drivers are very aggressive on the road and you have to hold on for dear life. One day I had a woman driver, Luva, and she was the best I had met. We had a great chat for 20 minutes, and before I left I asked for her number (so that I could call her for future taxi services!) She told me there are only about 20 female taxi drivers in the whole country.

I have been here long enough to pick out the "private taxis." When I was young in Hong Kong, I always wondered how people knew which of the unmarked cars were for hire. Now I have gotten the hang of it. One guy was particularly good (i.e. he drives safely and speaks Spanish clearly) and he picks up passengers right around where I live. I got his number also.

Does The System Need Changes?

While the system is a real problem for newcomers, it's working for the locals; otherwise, a change would have already been made. I personally think it's a charming way of denoting addresses, albeit often frustrating. From the economic point of view, a change will save the country a lot of time. As is, people are wasting a lot of time and money delivering bills, merchandise, etc. Everything takes longer than it really should. More importantly, once in a while I see an ambulance flying down the street, and I only hope that they know exactly where they are going. As you can imagine, without named streets, there are no GPS systems in the automobiles in this country. My hand-held GPS shows me the Pan American highway and a few major highways between the provinces. If you are a new driver in this country, it's pure trial and error in learning your way around. As charming as this system may be, a change will save the country a lot of money and frustration in the long run, and possibly even a few lives.

19. Extra!

March 1, 2005 - San Jose, Costa Rica

The Ultimate Four Letter Word: Sick

I am interrupting the regular journalizing to bring you the latest development on my health. Ever since my arrival in Costa Rica at the end of November, I have been sick quite often, and it almost always happened on the weekends. The symptoms range from your typical allergy effects to a sore throat, losing my voice, body-aches, feeling listless, a headache, and hearing echoes. The strange thing is that during the week I am fine, and when Friday comes, one or more of the symptoms start to appear. I have visited Costa Rica about 10 times between 1999 and 2004 and was never once sick. Nevertheless, when I planned this sabbatical, being sick in a foreign land was one of my biggest concerns, the other being underestimating the cost of a sabbatical year.

Understandably, I was fully expecting a healthy 11-day visit to the US when I was there in the middle of February. My plan had me arriving in Dallas on a Friday, thinking that I would cleverly avoid another "weekend sickness" just in time. I should have known better than to push my luck though. Everything was fine, initially. On Saturday, I went out to dinner with a friend. With the second bite of my dinner, I started to cough, and 3 bites later, I completely lost my voice and couldn't eat anymore. My friend and I ordered the same thing - Pho (Vietnamese noodle), so I couldn't blame the food as he ate the whole thing without a hitch.

The 5 days spent in Dallas were productive - tax was filed, every meal was organized with some business or personal friends so no time was wasted, really. All my friends were very kind and generous to pick up the tab; I really appreciate that. Then I went to my southern parents' home by the lake outside of Birmingham, Alabama. As usual, we had a great visit. In the middle of the second night, (it was a Friday; coincidence? I think not!) my stomach had a riot and refused to house the dinner any longer. And I had a chill at that moment. While I was porcelain worshipping, a fainting sensation hit me. It was the night the cold front went through and it was in the low thirties outside. Thinking that if I must pass out, I would be better off being in the warm bed than lying half-naked on the cold stone floor, so I suspended the worship and started to head back to bed. Didn't make it.

My right forehead hit the ground first, and then my shoulder and chest. I hit so hard that the impact aroused me (as in the impact woke me, versus the other meaning of "arouse"). I felt my face on the cold floor and told myself that I had to get back to bed or Helen and Vance would find a dead body in their basement the next morning. It's possible that I remained unconscious on the floor for very long, but I don't recall that. I spent the rest of the night in bed, fighting the urge to return to the porcelain worship by remaining completely motionless, vowing to live a fuller and more responsible life if I should still find myself alive at daybreak, wondering how to alert Helen and Vance of my incident (crawling upstairs was not an option), and contemplating the flight back to Dallas in seven hours time.

Miraculously, I survived the night without making any further mess. I walked upstairs and found Helen and told her what happened. That's when I found out about the scratched face and the bumps on my head. Now that someone in the house knew, I felt safer to go back to sleep. A hot shower and voluntary porcelain worship again did wonders and I actually felt well enough to fly back to Dallas. By the time I landed in Dallas, I almost felt normal, except for the hunger. I felt more or less fine the rest of the weekend and decided to take the original flight to Miami on Monday as planned, chalking it up as a 12-hour bug.

When David, one of my colleagues, met me at the airport, I had no other symptoms than a sore upper right torso, up to the forehead. It was Monday after all, the traditional day to get better for me. David himself didn't have as much luck. He had been sick himself the whole weekend. I sat in on one of his meetings, which brought a lot of mixed emotions - I forgot how difficult consulting work can be, and all I remember is the fun side. A group of us went to dinner. All was fine, except for David and his cold. Camping out on his soft couch that night brought renewed pain to my chest, but it wasn't bad enough to stop me from returning to Costa Rica last Tuesday. Still I couldn't help wondering if I would catch the cold that David had.

I felt good enough that I went to work on Wednesday and Thursday. On Friday, Alvaro and I went to the telephone company to fix my cell phone password and ran a few errands. We ended up spending 4-5 hours in town. While in town, I started to cough again. What should I expect? It was Friday after all! But coughing brings renewed pain to my sore and bruised ribs. So I decided to stay home instead for the rest of the day, thinking that it would be time to see a doctor if this ridiculous weekend sickness lasted the whole weekend. I did not leave the bed on Saturday and stayed in it most of Sunday. And I was feeling almost normal by the end of Sunday. But I decided a visit to a doctor would finally be in order. But which one?

Doctoring, The Tico Way

My tico family secured a doctor's name and his two phone numbers for me on Sunday night. They tried to describe to me where the doctor's office was. It was a frustrating exercise for both (remember the address system?). On Monday morning, I called the two numbers - one was a fax and the other one was a wrong number. The telephone directory said that the doctor's name was not listed. I was in no mood to see the humor at that time.

I put on a clean shirt and went to look for a taxi. None was around but the bus was arriving. Unfortunately, the bus exhaust and the uneven ride brought quite a nauseous and dizzy sensation. It was only a 10-minute ride and it was sheer will power that I didn't mess up the bus. The doctor's office was closed. It was 10:30 in the morning. No posted office hours either. A few Spanish curse words would have been very handy, but I have been refusing to learn them all these years to make sure I sound like a gentleman in Spanish at all times.

Next door was a pharmacy. There is something wonderful here in Costa Rica. Instead of a registered pharmacist, most pharmacies have a certified doctor on staff to dole out medical advice. They don't do examinations, but they will listen to your problems and advise on medicine to take. For free.

I asked for the doctor and started to explain my problems to her. She advised that I should be examined by a doctor instead of getting over-the-counter advice, and the nearest doctor was 300 meters away. I wasn't sure if I could walk the 300 meters, but it was downhill and I got myself in the doctor's office without further incident. A black man in a white coat (turned out he was the doctor himself) was sitting at the reception desk reading the newspaper, and I thought I looked rather sickly by then and was surprised to find myself needing to explain to him that I was there for consultation. Did he think I was there selling encyclopedias? At the same time, I started to worry about two things - what kind of doctor he might be, playing both doctor and receptionist, and if he spoke any English. Whatever it was, I didn't have the energy to go anywhere else.

He was actually a bit embarrassed by the situation and went to find the receptionist, and then he retreated to his office. She took my name, date of birth, and phone number. I quietly asked her if the doctor spoke English. Más o menos. More or less. I have learned that it is a polite way to mean "not really."

I realized then that whether I would get better or worse after this consultation would be a result of how well I could explain my medical situation in Spanish. Fortunately, if that's the right word, I have been sick often enough here to pick up the Spanish words to describe my symptoms. He called me in his office. There was no nurse. He took my temperature (37 Celsius) and my blood pressure (110/80) and all I could think was that this was the first time a doctor performed these services on me. He was pleased with the vital signs.

As I told him the symptoms, he started to give me medicine to take right there. He decided that I had a virus, and sprayed my throat with something. I asked him what it was and didn't get an answer. I talked about passing out and how it happened once before 5 years ago due to a stomach virus. He gave me two more pills. I complained about chest pain when I coughed. He looked for the very spots by asserting pressure on my chest. After I said no for the first attempts, he started to punch me instead. When he found the first spot, I swear I almost hit him back. I held his arms with both my hands. He found a total of three spots and proceeded to give me injections on my chest in four different areas. The pain did subside and I asked him what was in the syringe, but all he did was smile and proceeded to shake my hand. I felt like I just bought a pair of Timberland's from my favorite shoe salesman at Macy's in Dallas.

I had to lie down for those injections. When I returned to a vertical position and sat down at his desk again, he gave me a spoon of magnesium milk for the dizziness. That was last thing I took there. Then I wondered: if I told him I was hungry, would he give me a sandwich there?! I was thinking by now how much it would cost me. I asked the receptionist earlier and she said the consultation would cost 9,000 colones, right at about $19.99. Now that I was feeling better, I started to look around and found his credentials on the wall. To my relief, he graduated from The University of Costa Rica and took a two-day Continuing Education course at Harvard Medical School last March. I will write more about the university system here in a separate entry. He recommended blood, urine, and what-not types of analyses to make sure I didn't have something more serious, considering my faithful weekend sicknesses. The whole visit cost 11,000 colones, or less than $25, and we spent quite a while together.

He also prescribed 5 different medications for my problems. On the prescription, he specified the exact time for each medication, and I found that a very nice personal touch. For instance: Valvirex: 8am 5pm. Zithromax: 6pm. Because of these specific time instructions, I have to set my alarm and carry a card to remind me of what time to take which medication. Meanwhile, I was satisfied that I went through this consultation mostly in Spanish and he had no trouble understanding me.

Lab Work

The Lab was in the city of Guadalupe, 75 meters east of the National Bank of Costa Rica - that's the address! I don't know why but you are not supposed to eat breakfast the morning they draw blood for analysis. I followed their rules anyway. On Tuesday, I showed up at 7am for the blood work because I would have drunk water by 8am as the first medication was due. The technician told me that the results would be ready by 5pm that same day. Speaking of efficiency!

I had a clean bill of health - no parasite, blood contents were as normal as can be. In fact, the microbiologist was amazed how "healthy" my results were, and proceeded to comment on how good my Spanish was, as if they were related events - unfortunately, I can't agree completely on both counts. But they are both getting better. It's only the midweek yet; I can still afford to be a little cocky.

I am feeling much better now, though still a bit weak. I resumed my teaching today and will have another class tomorrow. Meanwhile, I am also determined to be "healthy" this weekend. We shall see. Thanks for reading this extra-long Extra!

20. Life's Guarantee And Surprise

March 9, 2005 - San Jose, Costa Rica

I write this entry with utmost sadness.

I asked for and expected all kinds of experiences in this sabbatical year. Going to a new friend's funeral in Costa Rica was NOT one of them.

One of the colleagues at the church and I became fast friends. She has been extremely nice and helpful to me since my arrival. She guides me through the cultural mines of working in a different cultural setting. I help her with fine tuning her already very good English and using the computer. She teaches 7th grade Spanish, as a volunteer, in the evening school for adults who want to finish high school. The church offers these classes free to the community. And she invited me to one of her classes a few weeks ago.

That evening, I met her husband. He came to pick her up after school was over. It was very clear that this couple really loved each other and respected each other. They gave me a ride home and we had a good chat and talked about going to the famous Chinese restaurant one of these weekends. He worked as a body guard for a local businessman.

Monday afternoon, a phone call came to the office. A gang of four people attacked the businessman and my friend's husband was shot while protecting his boss. The boss survived the attack. My friend's husband took down two of the attackers and injured another one during the process. Then he perished. He was 28. The incident was so violent that it made it to the news.

I found out about this on Tuesday morning when I got to the office. The service was to be held that afternoon and the burial took place right afterwards..Everyone from the church attended. .

When the coffin was lowered into the ground, I distinctly felt my friend's pain. Before the service, I learned that she was married once before in her early 20s, and her first husband died of cancer in his 20s. At the young age of 35, she is now twice widowed. What can you say to console someone who suffers such deep pain? Do words even exist that are appropriate and adequate for such sadness? My heart sank for her suffering.

Death, one of life's few guarantees, always comes as such a surprise.

21. At Home In Costa Rica II

> March 17, 2005 - San Jose, Costa Rica

Sick A Lot?

Like I said two entries ago, I seem to have been sick more often here – one thing after another, fortunately nothing too serious. My visit to Dr. Carranza two weeks ago resulted in me being free of most symptoms in these last weeks. Incidentally, I have discovered a whitish band on my left eye ball in these two weeks. It doesn't itch or hurt. Nor does it affect my vision in any way. To be on the safe side, I went to an ophthalmologist here in San Jose. Dr. Bernardo Rubinstein speaks better English than I do, which enabled the visit to go smoothly. He tested my vision and was surprised to find my eye in question has better than 20/20 vision.

It is a calcium deposit. It's not cancer and it's not an illness, so the doctor said. It normally results from trauma to the eye, which I have not endured. He said he had never seen anything like this before (meaning without the trauma). Since the deposit happens during Lasik surgery, that's not necessarily to say it was the result of the surgery, he suggested that I consult my eye surgeon on my next visit to Dallas, scheduled to be in late April. Meanwhile, he has no concern about it and told me not to lose sleep over it and not to mess with it with eye drops or anything else either. He told me to "keep an eye on my eye," to make sure the band is not growing. I wasn't sure if the pun was intended on that sentence. But I supposed he meant the good eye should look out for the calcium deposit. He also said the calcium deposit could be surgically removed, but there's no urgency to it at the moment. I took a picture of my eyeball so that I could scientifically compare the progress on a weekly basis. I am actually quite relieved. Overall, I am doing really well and there is nothing alarming. Still, all of these issues have encouraged me to inspect my life here.

My Oral Consumption

At home, I have been on a "carbohydrate diet"; that is, everything that I eat is high in carbohydrates. A typical local breakfast is called

Gallo Pinto - fried rice with beans and eggs, supplemented with tortilla and cheese. It's such an important local dish that MacDonald's offers McPinto for breakfast and Burger King answers that with its own BK Pinto. The locals drink a lot of delicious fresh fruit juices, which is great in itself, but they add loads of refined sugar in the preparation of the drink.

Doña Claudina is a very lovely old lady. Incidentally, she just turned 70 this year. Her 99 year-old mother lives in the countryside, and she is mentally still very alert. Doña Claudina is very easy to live with and she's very independent. Unfortunately, she speaks a form of Spanish that is very different from what I studied, and our communication is usually limited to, "Are you hungry?," "The food is delicious," "It's very cold today," or on rare occasions "It's not so cold today." Whenever she attempts to tell me something outside of these three lines in length, often times we both end up feeling like idiots. To be sure, we are getting better at this, slowly. She had a 3rd grade education (I am not criticizing and saying that's little because that's three years more than what both my parents have) and lived most of her life in the countryside, so her diction, colloquial phrases, and accent are a world away from my artificial and formal textbook Spanish.

Well, she communicates her love to us three boys through food. She calls us "chiquillos." It's the diminutive form of "chico," or boys. So, we are little kids in her eyes. We are fed great quantities, and often. It's almost like a cruise ship - fortunately she retires at 8:30 in the evening; otherwise, I honestly wouldn't know how to turn down the obligatory midnight buffet. All three of us can use some weight loss, but we are also sensitive not to hurt her feeling. It's quite a culinary dilemma that we have. Besides, I don't have much discipline. On top of that, Doña Claudina is afraid to use the gas stove top, so she prepares everything with an electronic frying pan.

Once, I opened my big mouth, surprise!, in an attempt to convince her that we are city boys and we don't work on the farms and our jobs require us to sit at a desk all day long, so we don't require as much food, i.e., calories, as farmers would. In order to make sure not to offend her accidentally, I confessed to her that I can only buy clothes, especially pants, in Hong Kong and I couldn't afford to stuff my mouth so much that I would need to buy larger-sized clothes while I am in Costa Rica. We three are exercising greater self control these days.

She has a very different schedule from the rest of us. She gets up very early and has breakfast, and then she starts cooking lunch at 8:30am and eats at 10:30am. I honestly don't know what time she cooks dinner, but whenever I come home early, say 5pm, she has already eaten dinner and the cooked food is left in the pan, covered, until we have dinner at 7pm, or later on some nights.

These days, during the week, I have reverted to cereal for breakfast. The weekend is not a weekend without gallo pinto! Lunch is at church - rice, some meat (chicken, pork, beef, etc.), some salad, and a natural fruit drink. Dinner at home is rather similar to that of lunch in terms of variety. My weight has been holding steady now that I am watching the quantity of input.

A Word About The Work - Slow

The funding of the server is still in the air. I remind them every now and then that I am out of here by the end of June, come hell or high water. So, if they really want to have a network, oh well, it's up to them now. Because of the absence of the server and the network, my priorities have switched slightly and I am putting in more time working on a Student Registration program for the church school. Ironically, this will also be running on the server eventually. You know, you simply can't do a software implementation project without the software, nor the network. Nonetheless, this is quickly becoming a full-time job for me. It's eating into my teaching preparation time.

I had two meetings with the software provider this week. At the first meeting, three of us from the church attended. We spent 15 minutes chit-chatting before we tended to the issues at hand. Ah, I am in Latin America now. It was quite fun to see this phenomenon. I had studied about this in college but have not had the opportunity to experience it first hand until now.

Talking about these things in Spanish really drains me. Also, programmers are often times not your best verbal communicators. They speak fast and softly. I had a three-hour training session with a programmer this morning at the software office, and I was exhausted and hungry afterwards. Instead of taking two buses, I took a taxi to return to the church for lunch. And the taxi driver wouldn't stop talking to me after he greeted me with the usual chino - China Man! I gave him the impression of listening to him by nodding at sporadic intervals. He then broke into singing! He sang songs in Hebrew (I had to ask). When we were approaching the church, he wanted my cell phone number because he wanted me to go to this Chinese church in town where he could set me up with some local Chinese women! I politely and firmly rejected his offer.

Should I be offended? Even a stranger taxi driver thinks that I need a more exciting social life! Isn't it the truth though?

22. Thoughts From Semana Santa (Holy Week)

March 30, 2005 - San Jose, Costa Rica

Costa Rica is definitely a Catholic country, even though Protestants are growing in great numbers. Unlike the US, last Thursday and Friday were official holidays here. Schools and government offices were shut down the whole week. Workers were sent home by Wednesday afternoon. However, most people took advantage of the holiday and took two and half days of vacation to make a nine-day holiday. As such, many small businesses were closed the whole week. San Jose was literally a ghost town on Thursday and Friday. I loved it; there was no traffic jam for a change.

Even though I was baptized Catholic, I haven't practiced Catholicism since leaving Hong Kong. I attend a much more progressive and liberal Protestant church in Dallas. When I first came down to San Jose, I went to mass and that hour spent at the church distinctly reminded me why I no longer practice Catholicism. While there is nothing wrong per se, it just does not meet my spiritual needs anymore. (Oh great, I talk about religion here and politics on the Potpourri page on the website, so if we throw in a turkey somewhere, we are ready for a family style Thanksgiving dinner. Let the fight begin!)

At any rate, I decided to go to church Friday. The tradition is that out of the year, people in Costa Rica do not drive on Good Friday. It's a day for the body and the soul to rest. I quite appreciate that token. There were the occasional cars (agnostics and "heathens" are abound), but there were no buses. We walked about a mile down hill to la Igelsia Católica del Carmen. It's a relatively small church. There were more people than there were seats. I figured I wasn't the only visitor that day.

Masses have a very established routine and there is really no need to print the "program" for the regulars. They all know what to say, when to say it, when to stand, when to sit and when to kneel. I can possibly do this in Cantonese without the cues, but English will be a major challenge and Spanish is downright impossible. Even though they tried to make this Good Friday mass dynamic, one gets the impression that the congregation just could not get excited.

When the mass was over, there was a procession. This happened in every church. They reenacted what happened two thousand years ago on Good Friday. The procession went on until late into the evening. It was quite a sight.

Many Catholic Costa Ricans are not following the Catholic traditions. This does not make them bad people. It's up to the Church to bring them back if they feel that it's their job to save the souls of the people. For instance, Gilberto and Alvaro claim to be agnostic, rather than Catholic. The beaches, hot springs, volcanoes and rain forests were filled with domestic vacationers. That Friday evening, a "heathen" friend of ours went shopping and invited us. A new store, called EPA, opened in March. It's like a Home Depot, even with its own local lesbian clientele. I was surprised, then rather disappointed, to find that the store chose not to observe the national tradition and instead stayed open with normal business hours on Good Friday. It was the only store, other than the occasional restaurants, that was open. On an unrelated note, alcohol was not sold in the stores on Thursdays and Fridays. People stocked up earlier in the week. Bars were still open though.

My opinion is that (here he goes....), while this is definitely a Catholic country, the number one religion is soccer, tightly followed by materialism. And when soccer season is out, materialism leads by a sizable margin, just like everywhere else in the world. I wouldn't be surprised if within a few years, when consumerism has a tighter grip on the culture, it would be an exception rather than the norm for stores to be closed during Holy Week. If you have any doubts, just look at Hong Kong. Well, I already expressed my sentiments in last year's newsletter.

I am not saying that it is wrong to long for better living conditions. In fact, I quite encourage it. I am afraid, however, that materials alone can only bring about physical comfort, but not happiness. Happiness comes from inside. We need a good balance of the two to be fulfilled. Failing to recognize this will only result in a void in our inner being.

23. Tico Life I

April 5, 2005 - San Jose, Costa Rica

Six months, or exactly half of this sabbatical, has passed. And I only have a couple of months left in Costa Rica, so it's high time I became prolific on this website production.

Cost Rica: The Richest Country In Central America

For those who may not be familiar with this region, Central America is comprised of Guatemala, Belize, El Salvador, Honduras, Nicaragua, Costa Rica and Panama. Mexico is, officially, part of North America; hence NAFTA (North America Free Trade Agreement) covers Canada, USA, and Mexico.

I won't bother to quote GNPs and per capita GDP, as they can be rather meaningless if wealth is not relatively evenly distributed, which is the case in the vast majority of the countries in the world, except the Scandinavian countries and less than a handful of other developed countries. Costa Rica is arguably the wealthiest country in Central America, though Panama will certainly have something to say about this assertion.

My tico friends (multiple sources) told me that manual labor workers and high school graduates make about $300 a month. Fresh college graduates make about $500, which is about what teachers make, maybe slightly higher. A lawyer friend told me that a lawyer, with years of experience, makes about $1,000, which is considered a very good income locally. A doctor working for a government hospital can bring in as much as $2,500 while a resident brings in $1,500, according to my lawyer friend. These are not official figures, but I have heard them enough times to trust their validity. Something baffles me.

I live and work among the locals. And I take the bus almost on a daily basis. The way the people dress themselves most certainly does not reflect this income level. When I look at how the people dress, I can't help but ask myself how in the world these people dress so respectfully. One book I read suggests that in this part of the world, dressing sloppily equals being poor, and people avoid presenting themselves in that light, whereas their counterparts in the wealthier countries dress like bums to "express themselves." Walking down the streets in San Jose or in a mall here will spare anyone the ridiculous sight, as commonly found in US cities, of young men wearing their pants so low that they are practically mooning the public.

People have credit cards. In line with the income, the credit limits are somewhere between $500 to $2,000, for the majority of the cardholders. And people do incur credit card debts - the worst kind of debt one can have as far as I am concerned. It's literally financing the past with the future. The American style of advertising is quickly becoming commonplace here also. I hear this in Spanish advertising often: You deserve this vacation! Buy it now! No interest and no payment for 6 months! Your family has earned this lifestyle. On the other hand, I just don't see how some people live on their income. My tica family told me that some manual labor workers make $300 a month and that's the whole income for a family of four. I suppose one eventually learns to cope with the lot they have found themselves in. And these are not the ones who carry a few credit cards in their wallets.

My tica family took the car to a car wash this Sunday and we chatted with the guy who washed the car. In this place, washing the car is ALL done manually. For a little less than $9, they deep wash your engine with (high pressure) water, wash the floor mats, thoroughly vacuum and clean the car inside and out, and wax it. It took almost an hour. We chatted with the guy who did the job, a young man from Nicaragua, and learned that he works 12 hours a day, 6 days a week, for about $13 a day. He then earns 10% (of the car wash price) for each car he washes. I should be ashamed to feel that washing my car by hand once every 3 months was a drag. I bet he prays for sunny days. The rain season starts in a few months and if it is anything like the US, people don't wash their cars as often when it rains.

On the other extreme of the economic spectrum, there are brand new Mercedezes and BMWs running around town. I went to Multi Plaza, "the best" mall in San Jose over the weekend to see how the rich shop in Costa Rica and found Versace, Da Vinci (furniture and decorations), several stores selling plasma TVs, and multiple lifestyle stores for home decorations, among others. I like the bookstore the best. Unfortunately, most books are shrink wrapped.

The Immigrants' Dilemma

Costa Rica borders Nicaragua to the north. Rio San Juan (St. John River) serves as a natural border. The population of Costa Rica is roughly four million, a million or so of which are of Nicaraguan origin.

I always feel that it is the (illegal) immigrants who keep up the economy. They are the ones who take on jobs at minimum wage that the natives hesitate to take. Maybe they can't afford to take them? Some people complain about immigrants while they are taking advantage of the cheap labor. This is true in most countries that have a poorer neighbor. In the case of Middle East countries, they bring them in from Sri Lanka, India, the Philippines, etc. That's what I remember from my visit to Bahrain in 1986.

The same happens here. The difference is that there is generally no language barrier, which makes it much easier for the new immigrants to move into the mainstream society. The construction sites are filled with Nicaraguans (known as nicas in Spanish). They are also the ones who take up house cleaning jobs and jobs at the car wash, i.e., lowly paid manual labor. People generally contribute the rising crime rate to the influx of immigrants from the neighbor to the north. Granted, three nica brothers held up a bank in Monteverde, a town a few hours from San Jose, last month and killed 8, 9 people during the 48-hour horror. This certainly didn't help matters. One time I saw some graffiti in a neighborhood, spray painted in large letters "Nicas go home". I wonder what this does to the psyche of a young nica. Well, if they are born here, they are technically ticos, not nicas.

While we outsiders tend to think of Central America as a homogeneous block, the reality is that they can find a lot of differences among themselves in spite of their common language. I haven't been to Nicaragua yet, but if a $300 a month job attracts them to abandon their roots and family to cross the river, I can only imagine what they were leaving behind.

I think, for economic reasons more than anything else, Costa Rica identifies itself more with Panama, the neighbor to the south, than with Nicaragua. After all, both countries claim to be the Switzerland of Central America, albeit for different reasons. Panama fancies itself as Switzerland for its banking system, while it's the political neutrality, relative peace, and the absence of a military force that causes Costa Rica to make that claim.

According to one study, there are more than 100,000 Chinese in Costa Rica. >100K!! The majority of them are from China and some from Taiwan. Costa Rica is one of the 13 or so countries that have an official diplomatic relationship with Taiwan, i.e., Costa Rica recognizes Taiwan as an independent country. The Chinese in Costa Rica mostly run neighborhood corner stores and Chinese restaurants. *One* of them goes around town with a laptop computer in his backpack and tries not to be conspicuous. First generation immigrants have the distinct reputation of having a hard time learning Spanish. The double R trill is a killer. Rrrrrrrrr.

Once in a while I trek down hill from the church to the Mini Super Montero for a diet Coke. The Mini Super is owned by a Chinese family. On my third visit, they couldn't help their curiosity and asked me what I was doing there. The grandmother has been there for 15 years and speaks enough to do the simple transactions in Spanish and nothing else. The two youngsters in their late teens or early twenties, seemingly brother and sister, arrived less than 3 months ago. I couldn't figure out how they are related to the older lady. They are learning Spanish but already want to go back to China. Everybody envies the economy in China, so why are they coming to Costa Rica? Anyway, when the grandmother found out that I work in the church/school, she asked me to help her inquire about enrolling her 4-year-old-Costa-Rica-born-Chinese grandson. And I agreed to translate for them when the boy registers for school. The poor boy speaks half Chinese and half Spanish, not truly fluent in either.

After talking with the school administrator, I reported to them that the child can be accepted in midyear for pre-kindergarten. The grandmother told me that her daughter is now reluctant to put the child in school, citing that he doesn't speak enough Spanish to go to school yet. What does she think will be required of the child? To give a speech to the school on day one? It's pre-kindergarten, for crying out loud! I told them the obvious - that's why the child should be at school, to LEARN. The youngsters shrug their shoulders. The grandmother looked at me, feeling embarrassed that she wasted my time on the inquiry. I said good-bye to them, trekked up hill back to the church, sipping another diet Coke, feeling sorry for the kid that I had never met, and being thankful that my parents didn't hesitate to put me in school.

24. I Worry About You?!

April 8, 2004 - San Jose, Costa Rica

Estoy Preocupado Por Ti

First of all, I am fine. Really.

Well, I have had this nagging pain on my right wrist for a few weeks. It comes and goes. Then it decided to stay. I finally went back to see Dr. Carranza again. I told him that both his corrective and preventive medicines worked well on my general health. I haven't lapsed into weekend sickness. When I passed out in Alabama back in February, I landed on my right side, and hurt my right wrist among other parts. Much of the pain was suppressed by other more prevalent symptoms at that time and I almost forgot about it, until these last few weeks. After I told the good doctor of my complaints, he said:

"Estoy preocupado por ti!" or *I worry about you!*

It's not the tone that I didn't like. It's the words themselves. Should a doctor be allowed to tell his patient that? Such words could have sent some mentally fragile patients – I am slowly getting there – over the edge! The X-ray taken at Jerusalem Christian Hospital indicated that nothing was broken. He requested a written analysis from them, but they didn't follow his instructions. So, I have been going back and forth between the hospital and the doctor's office the whole week. The report was finally delivered to the doctor, by me, in person, on Friday - I was either at the doctor's or the hospital, or both, every day of the week. No wonder I am tired this week.

Here's the original report:

    RESULTADO

    En el presente estudio se observa una adecuada mineralización osea.

> Los diferentes huesos de carpo mantienen una relación anatómica conservada sin que se evidencien alteraciones articulares ni tampoco imágenes que sugieran proceso neoplásico, traumático ni infeccioso.

Or what we would say in English in Texas: Everything is fiiiiiine.

Because of my health conditions during my months here, I have accidentally become pretty good at basic medical terms in Spanish. An unexpected bonus, if you will.

He suspected that I might have torn a tendon and sprained my wrist, so he gave me a Celebra (anti-inflammation pill) on the spot. I will need to take this thing for the next 10 days, and I will have to put this cream on, wrap it with bandage and take the anti-inflammation pill. He also ordered me not to lift anything for 30 days. I may finally have to use the porter service at the airports when I go to Dallas in a few weeks' time.

During the examination, he started to ask me about how long I have lived here, and how much longer I plan to stay (one can easily interpret that as: Do you want to live or what?) He doesn't understand why my health breaks down so often the way I do. Nor do I. I told him I grew up in much harsher environment than this. So it might have to do with aging. He then proceeded to ask me, while wrapping up my wrist, about the political situation in China and Hong Kong and Taiwan and how Hong Kong is doing since the transfer of sovereignty (soberanía, where in the world did I learn this word in Spanish?). For some odd reasons, my doctors in Dallas also ask me these questions, as if my being Chinese automatically qualifies me to opine on these issues intellectually. Anyway, we had a good chat. He only charged me once for the three times that I saw him this week. He just wanted to be 100% sure that nothing serious is cooking in me. At that point, I suddenly wondered how the local Chinese (the ones who don't speak Spanish, or English for that matter) see a doctor here. They find one who speaks Chinese? Where? I have only seen one doctor with a Chinese last name and he's a dentist. Even then, if he's a local born Chinese, there's no guarantee that he speaks Chinese, or more precisely, the specific dialects that the patients speak.

I looked around the office and saw his University of Costa Rica diplomas again, which reminded me to write about the education system here as I promised when I wrote the Extra! entry, which was what I was going to write. But I digressed. Big time.

Oh, in case you wonder, the calcium deposit on the eye is not growing. Thank the Almighty!

25. Tico Education System

April 18, 2005 – San Jose, Costa Rica

I didn't officially research this topic. I picked up this knowledge from multiple conversations with the locals. Don't hold me responsible for the accuracy. I suggest that you read this as if you were watching a 24 hour news channel. You should expect about the same level of accuracy.

Costa Rica is proud of its higher than 90% literacy rate. It has the most literate population among the Central American countries. That's a fact.

Because of the large Catholic population, there are obviously a lot of Catholic schools in this country. Some are private, but a lot are subsidized, i.e., the government pays the church to run the schools and the parents make up the difference. There are also plenty of private schools, most of which are "bilingual in English and Spanish," some "French and Spanish." The private schools could be Catholic, Christian (non-Catholic), or free of religious affiliation. Since this is a Catholic country, no one would make a fuss if the public schools teach religion. In fact, you would expect that every public school teaches it. However, to my dismay, students are not exposed to religions other than Roman Catholicism in public schools. Private schools are fair game.

On a personal note, I went to a very Catholic high school in Hong Kong. The campus itself is also a monastery. There's also a church, not just a chapel, on campus. It enrolls only boys. You can't get much more Catholic than this. We had "Religious Studies" for each grade. And we had Social Studies where we were free to explore and learn about other world religions, from the traditional Chinese religions to Islam, including the concepts of agnosticism, atheism, and evolutionism. The priests in my school were not threatened. Nor were the Christians in Hong Kong. So, for the life of me, I don't understand why certain segments in America (and to an extent, in Costa Rica) are so scared to expose their children to religious beliefs other than that of their own, be they religious or atheistic. And why would they want to send their children to school with the goal that the kids end up being ignorant and intolerant in a certain area?

(Perhaps they want the children to be just like themselves. Scary thought!) Ignorance and intolerance of differences are the roots of most evil acts around the world. OOPS, I digressed. Again.

Elementary And High Schools

Back to Costa Rica. One year of kindergarten is required before one can be admitted to elementary school, which lasts 6 years. Then there is high school. There's no such concept as middle school. If you are in a technical program, high school lasts 6 years. For most people, it's 5.

Unless you are in a bilingual school, everybody takes 5 years of English and 3 years of French as foreign languages. Judging from my experience with the locals, I can't say the schools are very successful with their language education, not unlike Hong Kong. In Denmark, the Danish kids SPEAK English quite well after 2 years of English, but this is not true for Costa Rica. I don't know if Danish is closer to English. Maybe if they stop dubbing the TV programs into Spanish, the people will have more incentive to learn English. I imagine that the average number of students in a classroom may have something to do with the different results, as well as the teachers' command of the English language.

There are a large number of bilingual schools, with the majority being English and Spanish. The kids learn everything in English, except the Spanish language, and maybe civics and Costa Rican history. The youth minister at the church where I volunteer went to a French bilingual school. So, he learned everything in French instead of English. He also learned English as a second language. When I inquired why anyone would choose to have French fluency over English these days, the explanation I got was that they have a better chance of getting a scholarship for higher education in France.

Bachillerato Por Madurez

I understand that, in elementary and high school, you have to pass every subject before moving on to the next level. Along with other socioeconomic reasons, this causes drop-outs. And there are programs for these drop-outs, mostly adults, and sometimes youngsters who can't go to normal day schools for whatever reasons, so that they can obtain their high school diploma equivalency -

bachillerato por madurez - or roughly translated *mature diploma*. This is just like the GED in the US.

In the past, you took only one exam in each of the six core subjects and if you passed them all, you got your diploma. The rules have changed in recent years. You now have to pass each subject by grade, just like one would in the normal day school. From what I can see, this change has its advantages and disadvantages. The process definitely can take longer for most people. However, depending on where you dropped out of school, this new process actually makes it easier for some adults to finally get that diploma.

Imagine if you dropped out of school in the sixth grade, you would have to learn everything between the 6th-11th grade to take that exam in one shot. Even though you are a mature adult now, it could still be a daunting task, bearing in mind that most people drop out because studying was too challenging for them when they were younger. Many evening programs cater to the needs of this group of adults. The church where I work offers these courses free of charge. Since they are adults, the material for an academic year is condensed into a 4 month period. The government offers the exams once every four months. The students can take all six subjects in one shot, or one at a time, or any combination desired. They will be allowed to take the exams for the next grade only after they have passed all the subjects for the previous grade. So, realistically, for people who never went to high school, they can obtain their diploma in less than 2 years if they pass every exam in each subject every four months. This will also mean that they will be in school every night of the week and Saturday as well. Hard work, but possible.

Higher Education

This is the sector that interests me the most. This is a small country by any standard - 4 million people. There are more than 40 universities (or degree granting institutions) in this country.

There are four public universities and they are highly competitive - University of Costa Rica (UCR - arguably the most prestigious), National University, Cartago Institute of Technology, and University of Distance Learning (like an Open University in the commonwealth system, I suppose). Then there is this huge array of private universities, almost all of which offer these four disciplines:

Education, Business Administration, Psychology and Law. The bigger ones may also offer Medicine, Dentistry, Architecture, Nursing, Science, etc. Other ones specialize in Psychology or Law only. There are no university hospitals; all the teaching is done on campus, and the practice done in public hospitals. I once heard that it can be difficult for a non-UCR medical student to find a hospital to carry out residence.

While my local friends strongly disagree with me, I think higher education is very cheap here, especially public education. UCR costs less than $300 a year on the average. The local newspaper once ran a story, in January this year, stating that 30% of the people drop out of the public universities because they can't afford the tuition or they chose to hold a full time job instead. Maybe I was wrong after all, but I still want to see how they arranged their priorities and decided they *could* afford to drop out.

Private universities, depending on size and reputation, and discipline, may charge $1,000-2,000 a year. Some of these schools are very small. For instance, Isaac Newton University has one building of two stories and maybe 4-5 classrooms. Well, most of them have one building, albeit a bigger one, say 4-6 stories.

I also notice that most students at the private schools are working full-time and studying full/part-time. Understandably, $1000 a year can be a lot of money for some, especially for those who don't have a degree. I generally find that the Costa Ricans are quite eager to earn that sheepskin. And they sacrifice a lot for it - in terms of money and time. This seems to be the pattern in developing countries.

One thing that I don't see offered much in the private schools (they advertise weekly in the local paper) is liberal arts education. So, if you want to major in Performance Arts, English, Spanish, or History, you must fight yourself into one of the public institutions. I suppose when money is tight, you just can't afford to learn something simply because you love it. Otherwise, you will end up joining Garrison Keillor (in Prairie Home Companion, NPR) in the Association of English Majors.

26. Medical Week

April 23, 2005 24,000 Feet Above The Caribbean

I knew Life's Scenic Lookout was the theme of the sabbatical, but I never did expect the sub-theme to be *getting sick when you are not too busy*. Okay, I still insist it is not life-threatening. It definitely is uncomfortable, at times painful, but definitely not life-threatening. Even though I have been getting medical advice in Costa Rica, it is imprudent on my part not to see my regular doctors back home about my condition.

Medical Week (April 25-29)

So, I decided to get efficient, and called my ophthalmologist, dentist, and general practitioner a few weeks ago and lined up the appointments all for the same week. So, this week the eye doctor will check out the calcium deposit, which, by the way, is not growing and not bothering me the least bit. My dentist's family happens to provide me with temporary housing while I am in town in Dallas, so I might as well have my filling done, though it can wait until later in the year. Like the Hong Kong people would say, while you are so close to the Wong Tai Sin Temple ... (you have to be a Hong Konger to get this one, sorry). And the latest development, tendonitis, is slowly spreading to the left hand. I have an appointment with my general practitioner as well. I successfully navigated through the San Jose Airport (in Costa Rica, not California!) a few hours ago. Careful planning of the luggage weight distribution and modern day luggage design did help a lot.

Well, if I am flying all this way home, and I have been paying for my own health insurance during the last six months via COBRA, I feel it's only right that I should have a physical with my primary care provider as well. So, this will also take place this week. There you have it, four appointments in one week. It's medical week, don't you think?

At this very moment, I am on my way home, via Miami. When one is homeless like myself, albeit temporarily and self-inflicted, to say *I am going home* is a very interesting thought. Home definitely means more than just a physical place for me. It is also a concept. And a feeling. Hong Kong is home. So is Dallas. At the moment, strange enough, so is San Jose. My life there is more stable, i.e., I have a routine there, more so than anywhere else at the moment. Saying a temporary good-bye to the folks at the church yesterday was a bit emotional. It shall be interesting to see how it feels in June.

"Don't Touch My Balls!"

I heard the Physical Ed teacher, a Costa Rican young man, said this to his lower grade students this week. I was walking back to my office after lunch and walked by the class. I almost wet my pants right there.

Well, this is how tricky English can be. I thought it was classic linguistic humor. You just have to maintain a sense of humor when it comes to learning and dealing with foreign languages. Of course, what he obviously meant was "Don't touch THE balls; *i.e., leave them alone, in the box.*"

27. Notes From Dallas

April 29, 2005 Dallas, Texas

Miami does not make it to my list of favorite cities. The combination of heat and humidity is my biggest complaint. Too much like Hong Kong in that regard. However, when the Airbus landed in Miami, I was ready to kiss the ground.

As insane as the Miami International Airport may be (it's under major reconstruction), there is still that sense of order that I generally miss in Central America.

The Value Of Traveling

In my opinion, everyone should go travel and see at least a little of the rest of the world. I understand that not everyone can afford it. However, for a good portion of the people in the first world, it's a matter of priorities. I was making $250 a month when I took a 17-day trip from Hong Kong to London, Denmark and Bahrain (in the Middle East) at the age of 21. It's an extreme example, but it is possible. Besides, you wouldn't be going to Bahrain these days. Granted, I was anything but cool. I looked like I could get a ticket from the fashion police on any given day and I didn't have any of the cool toys of the epoch (like a 1.5 pound Walkman). But, I still have that experience with me. Where's their Walkman?

Traveling has many benefits. Personally, it's gratifying to know that whatever I experience in my travels, they stay with me for the rest of my life. No flood, hurricane, tornado, robbery, not even tsunami, if you must question, can take that away from me. It will only lose its value when I lose the only thing that's even more valuable - life itself.

Whenever I come back to the country after a visit to a foreign land, I appreciate what is available here much more. The drinking water is relatively safe. The streets are mostly free of potholes. And the Dallas drivers are, in general, a bunch of folks who are rather courteous to their fellow motorists. And the abundance of cheap Americanized Chinese food. And a language that I almost understand completely. Despite the TV news, I feel very safe here. If everyone gets to experience this feeling (not just knowing it intellectually by comparing arbitrary statistics such as the GNP and the cost of living), we, for one, will not have to put up with youngsters (and some adults) screaming *it's not fair*. Of course it's not fair, WE GOT the long stick! And we will see the absurdity of what makes headline news in this country.

Incidentally, the only times I don't feel this way is when I return from Denmark and Hong Kong. I just love Denmark. I might have been a Viking in one of my previous lives. Hong Kong is my hometown and a very developed city; my only problem is that I cannot see myself working as hard as those people do.

Unfortunately, some people travel and they bring America with them, and they incessantly complain when things don't work the way they are accustomed to. Well, come to think of it, not much unlike what I have been doing here on this journal.

So, if you can afford it, go travel. How in the world did I end up lecturing people here?!

Summary On The Medical Tour

Well, here I am in Dallas, 5 medical appointments in 5 days. They are behind me now, but it's one record that I don't look forward to breaking.

First of all, I went to my ophthalmologist on Monday. The lasik surgery last year gave me a stable 20/20 vision. I didn't think I would be comfortable not wearing glasses on a regular basis. Now, I don't remember what it was like wearing glasses for 24 years.

The alleged calcium deposit on my eye ball was, after all, a misdiagnosis. Dr. Evangelista said that calcium deposits only happen in the whites of the eyes, not in the cornea area. Now, I feel like getting a refund from Dr. Rubenstein in Costa Rica. He did charge me $50 for his work. What I have is degenerated cells in my cornea. These cells died from the lasik surgery and since they are not getting nutrition from the air, they are turning grayish white and will disappear on its own with time. I trust him more than the doctor in Costa Rica.

An hour later, I went to see my Primary Care Physician (PCP) about my wrist pain and he was rather intrigued by the medication that I brought from Costa Rica. After a brief examination, he referred me to a specialist as he saw something "interesting" in the X-ray that I brought from Hospital Cristiano Jerusalem. That was Monday.

The quick visit to the dentist reminded me of Extreme Makeover scenarios. The filling went smoothly. During the process, they used gas to keep me relaxed. It must be what I might feel like if I have a third beer. My record to date is one and half beers in the same evening and I already couldn't drive. I kind of look forward to having that third one after this experience.

This morning, I went to the bone specialist. He saw the X-ray and thought he saw something interesting also. He twisted and turned my wrist to look for the source of the pain. He was lucky I was in pain and hadn't had the third beer; otherwise, I would have shown him where he could find pain! Well, the examination went against his initial thoughts. He said he didn't know what was wrong with me. Maybe I am just self-centered, but I think I have heard that line a bit too often lately. He asked me what helped to alleviate the pain in the last month or so. So, in essence, I was prescribing medication for myself - a firmer splint, ice and Mobic. I have a tentative appointment with him again on May 20 - that's when we will decide if an MRI will be necessary to get to the bottom of the problem. I think this is probably the best thing to do for now - to give it more time to heal.

After that, I went back to my PCP for the physical. Everything is fine, except all these little things in the eye, knee, wrist and so on. After all, if my PCP is content, I am happy.

28. Crossing The Big Pond Again

May 1, 2005 Dallas, Texas

Changed Plan

I have never taken a cruise on the ocean. At the beginning of the sabbatical, I had planned to visit Hong Kong towards the end of the sabbatical year on a freighter. My plan was to cross an ocean by ship. By the time I had to book the trip in February (this kind of travel requires a lot more lead time and flexibility), I was not in the best conditions health-wise and the thought of being in the middle of the Pacific for 20 days without medical attention was too much to stomach. The rule is that the ship does not need to have a medical professional on board as long as there are less than 12 passengers. The container freighters, if they accept passengers, take on one to four passengers on the average. So, all you have is a first-aid box when you are crossing the ocean.

I started to look for alternatives.

Repositioning Cruise

The travel agent that handles this kind of travel also books people on a repositioning cruise. Mediterranean Shipping Company, headquartered in Genoa, Italy, has ships sailing in the Caribbean in the winter and in the Mediterranean in the summer. Hence, twice a year, they have to move the ships from one sea to another, crossing the Atlantic Ocean.

I found this 17-night repositioning cruise, on MS Lirica, from Port Everglade in Florida to Genoa in Italy for what seems to be a bargain. The ship will call at San Juan, St. Thomas, St. Lucia, Martinique, Barbados, Funchal (Madeira Islands), Malaga, Barcelona, and Genoa. I have no idea exactly what to expect and how to (or how not to) behave myself.

This kind of cruise is not what I had in mind at the beginning of the year, but I am sure I can make it work. All I am looking for are three meals a day, a private bathroom, a lot of time in the ocean, crossing an ocean in one piece, and staying dry. The cruise is from May 2-19. I shall write more about the journey as it unfolds, but I doubt that I will be able to update the website while at sea, though the ship has a cyber cafe for internet access and checking e-mail.

Homework For My Students

Before I left Costa Rica, I assigned some homework to my students. One item is to watch a set of DVDs that I left them so that they can keep practicing their listening and pronunciation skills during my month long absence. Helen and Vance (my southern parents) gave me the first season of Golden Girls on DVD when I visited them in February. As you may well be aware, this is my all-time favorite when it comes to sitcoms. Those early episodes gave me instant relief whenever I felt homesick in the last few months.

Before you think this is a crazy idea, you should know that this set of DVDs comes with English subtitles for hearing-impaired people. Therefore, the subtitles match the dialogs verbatim, and where appropriate, contractions are used as well. English is a very difficult language for nonnative speakers to pronounce in that the spelling and the sound of words are not perfectly correlated. The spelling serves only as a reminder for how the words are to be pronounced. The actual pronunciation comes from the phonetic symbols in the dictionaries. And I already taught them how to read the symbols during the last few months.

For the DVDs, I specifically instructed them to pay attention to the weak form of auxiliary verbs (e.g. can), the different pronunciation of "s" after voiced and voiceless consonants, as well as the pronunciation of past tense verbs, among other things that we have been studying together. It's hard for a foreigner to imagine, for example, that there's a "t" sound in the word "booked," while the letter "t" does not appear anywhere in the word.

I hope they find the series somewhat interesting. They have already been warned that understanding humor in a foreign language implies probably the highest level of comprehension, and they should take it as a challenge and not be frustrated by it.

Or, do you think I have completely lost my mind for incorporating Golden Girls into my lessons? More to come from the Atlantic.

29. Transatlantic I: Aboard MS Lirica

May 4, 2005 – The Caribbean Sea / Atlantic Ocean

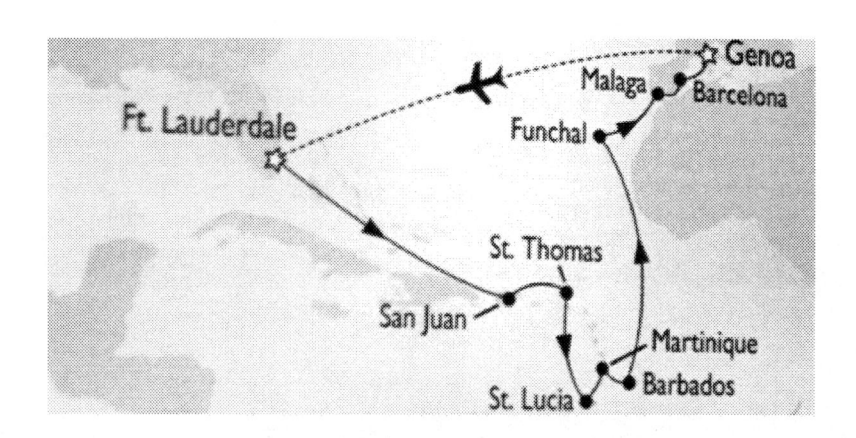

I suppose there's a scientifically defined border as to where the Caribbean ends and the Atlantic starts. Anyway, we (as in the sense of myself and the other fellow passengers and the crew) have been sailing for more than 44 hours nonstop from Ft. Lauderdale to San Juan, Puerto Rico. The sea was very calm yesterday but white caps are seen in all directions today. Today, one feels that one is on a ship. I am surprised that the ripples can push the ship to the extent that one can feel it. And I am excited to see the endless horizon for hours at a time. It's mesmerizing. I am sitting on the 12th deck, in the Blue Club (disco), by the window, while writing this entry. This is one of the quietest corners on the ship during the day.

Delayed Departure

There were some passengers arriving on a delayed flight to Miami. The ship waited for an hour for these passengers, which I think is very considerate of the ship. Granted, there's a good chance that the shipping company also booked these people's flight, so they may be obligated to wait.

While we waited that extra hour, a woman broke her leg on board, before we left port! A fire engine and an ambulance came. She was, along with all her luggage, taken off the ship. Even though she didn't miss the ship, she missed the cruise. I am not going to opine as to whether she's the lucky one or the rest of us are. We do have a long journey ahead of us and there are many nationalities on board. Any thing can happen still.

First Impression

I boarded the ship at about 12:30pm on Monday, May 2. That was the first time I used the elevator on board, and I have made a resolution not to use it again until disembarkation. I spent the first twenty-four hours learning the culture of cruise ship lifestyle. My initial impression is that this is "high school" for grown ups. What I mean is that the cruise director and his team work around the clock to keep people entertained, as if leaving the passengers alone would mean the risk of sabotage of the ship as the hooligans have to spend their energy somewhere somehow. Later on, I realized that keeping the passengers busy, i.e., away from their cabins, is a sure way to increase revenue for the ship. Alcohol sales go up, and there are more video/photo ops for the professional photographers if the passengers are participating in the activities. Though I think my *high school for grown ups* analogy still applies.

Though the ship has a capacity for 2,100 passengers, there are only 1,350 on board. This is really nice as there's never a very long line everywhere I go, including the midnight buffet. There are 730 crew members. The officers are all Italians. So far, I have met crew members from Italy, Slovenia, Bulgaria, Hungary, Honduras, the Philippines, Romania, England, Spain, Peru, and Madagascar, and the Asians are mostly Indonesians.

The passengers are almost as diverse as the crew. Announcements are made in English, Italian, French, German and Spanish, normally in this order too. And if it is an important message (like someone missing while the ship leaves port and during the evacuation drill), Dutch is also thrown in. The Cruise Director, Franco from Sardinia, Italy, can handle the first five languages very well all by himself. It's fascinating to see how fast he and his entertainment team can switch languages so effortlessly. These people are truly talented in languages. Compared with them, I am, at best, just a serious amateur.

There is a large group of Italian honeymooners on board. Florida Southern University (Lakeland, Florida) has a group of students taking the cruise, and taking 6 credit hours in two of these courses: Travel Journal Writing, Personal Finance (Travel), and Iberian Art History and Appreciation. They have classes a few hours a day while the ship is at sea and they will spend three weeks in Spain and Portugal as part of their course. What a way to earn six credit hours! And you think I am spoiled!

It's fairly safe to assume that, when you are 40, you are bound to be on the younger side of the passenger profile on most cruises, unless you are on a Disney cruise. I was talking to this couple from the States, and the husband commented that if I were a gigolo, I would do well on the cruise (because of the age thing). Doesn't that make you wonder what triggered that comment? I wasn't sure if I was supposed to take a better look at his wife or what.

The Food Culture

One thing I don't understand is the need to feed people 24 hours a day. There's food everywhere from 6:30am till after midnight. And during the night hours, there's room service if one must eat more. What have we done all day that will require such an intake of food? It's a real challenge for the weak-minded like myself when food is so readily available. Therefore, I made the decision to boycott the elevator service. Otherwise, excessive weight gain is imminent. Meanwhile, weight gain is a guarantee for this lifestyle. Funny though, there is not a single crew member that is not fit (OK, I saw that three were less than perfect in the restaurant). Do you suppose there is a rule that governs their weight like there is for the flight attendants on many airlines?

The food is generally very good, especially in the full service dining rooms. As far as I am concerned, the only way they can improve is to add a Chinese restaurant! I also learned that pasta is not the main course of an Italian dinner. It's just one of the courses, normally right before the entree.

The only thing even more available than food is alcohol. It's really a good thing that I don't drink (anymore); otherwise, the beverage bill might easily become more expensive than the passage itself. First thing in the morning around the pool deck, they push this little cart around with the sign "Eye Openers" on it. Screwdrivers and Bloody

Marys are the only names I recognize. Calling the drinks "Eye Openers" is very clever, I think, especially when one is drinking at eight in the morning.

Sun Damage?

You can generally tell who the regulars (to the cruise lifestyle) are from their skin condition (and sometimes body size, if they make one trip too many to the midnight buffet table). It's ironic that the Caucasians are risking skin cancer to get a tan and look darker; meanwhile, people of naturally darker complexion are doing everything in their power to lighten their skin. I remember Michael Jackson was once black. That's the power of marketing. There's no winner, except the companies who sell you these products that make your skin lighter or darker, depending on which side you find yourself on when you are born. It seems that the rule is that you can never be dark enough if you were born light, and you can never be light enough if you were born dark. It's just like the fashion magazines telling us that we can never be thin enough. Incidentally, as a child, I always enjoyed watching Popeye (in Cantonese), but I never understood why he picked Alice as his girlfriend. She's a bag of bones; I have seen scarecrows that have more meat! Maybe those two characters subscribe to the fashion magazines as well.

30. Transatlantic II: Caribbean Ports of Call

May 9, 2005 – Atlantic Ocean N16°10.374' W053°0.412'

Most people reading this know a whole lot more about cruises and the Caribbean than I do. I am only writing this to remind myself of the glimpses I had during the brief visits.

The Ports Of Call

San Juan, Puerto Rico - We arrived at 7 pm. After being at sea for 48 hours nonstop, it was a bit of relief to be on solid ground again. Well, the ground might have been solid, but the rocking sensation has sunk in and I was rocking just the same, ashore or aboard. There were night excursions organized, to my surprise. It was a perfect opportunity to get some forgotten personal items from Walgreen. These items are all available in the store aboard ship, but it's a monopoly, and the price tags reflect that reality. We left for St. Thomas at 2 am.

San Juan is a US territory. There are two schools of political thought here: to become the 51st state, or maintain the status quo. The latter seems to give them all the goodies, the military protection, the citizenship, the right to use the "Made in USA" label on their products, the freedom of not being a state, though they don't get congressional representation in the Senate. I am not sure about the House though. After visiting the other Caribbean islands, I have found that it's little surprise that not too many people are asking for independence.

Amalie Charlotte, St. Thomas - one of the US Virgin Islands. I did a three-hour bus tour, and I decided that I couldn't afford it anymore. It was way over-priced, $45 for 3 hours of three not-so-exciting stops. St. Thomas is a very quaint place. There's no river and no source of fresh water. All the fresh water comes from desalinating the sea water. As far as I am concerned, it is way too small an island for permanent dwelling. I like the Danish street names. This place was once ruled by the Danish Royal Crown. Though the names have been translated into English, the original Danish names are kept alongside the English names.

St. Lucia - It's obviously poorer than the previous two ports of call. The people seem quite friendly and content. The thing that really stands out in my mind is the students' uniforms. The shirts are very white and in good shape even at the end of the school day. The high school students look really calm and well-behaved, very different from the public schools in Dallas. If I saw them in an American high school, I would have to guess that Prozac was served at lunch. Another thing that I noticed is how fit the people are, and this is true on the other islands we visited as well. I didn't see anyone that can be classified as obese. A waiter at the pub told me that there is no university on this island. If they want to go to college, and if they can afford it, they most likely pick the US or the UK.

Port of France, Martinique - This is my favorite port in the Caribbean. I think the fact that this is the only non-English/Spanish speaking Caribbean destination for the ship makes me more aware of the surroundings. I explored downtown on my own. It was interesting to hear French among the locals. I witnessed a verbal fight on the way back to the ship. The expressions on the two men's faces were mad, but the language wasn't really meant to be yelled. It just doesn't have the yelling rhythm that Spanish or Cantonese offers for verbal fights.

Bridgetown, Barbados - This former British colony feels rather English. We got here on a Sunday. Shops, except those at the pier, were all closed. My kind of town. People dressed very well for the church services. I was afraid I would miss the ship, so I got back to the pier two hours before sailing. We were warned that if we missed the ship, the next time we could catch up would be six days later in Funchal. I suppose that when Lucy (I Love Lucy) missed her cruise and got flown in by helicopter, it was all for comic effect and doesn't really happen in real life.

When we left the port, we had a few false alarms involving passengers not making it to the ship in time for the sailing. As I travel alone, this was one of my biggest fears. I only had some cash and my camera with me when I went ashore. The ship kept everyone's passport (except the Europeans). I believe this is for immigration procedures, and I figure it also neatly serves as collateral for our expenditures aboard. When one couple was reportedly missing at Barbados, one of the officers left their passport copies with the port officials, and supposedly they had to fly to Funchal (how?) to catch up with the ship 5 days later. It turned out it was a "swiping error" and no one was missing. I heard that people have been left behind before.

One common theme on these islands is that there are plenty of shops selling gold and diamonds. Maybe the frequent cruisers can tell me if these are supposed to be good bargains. And many of these shops are run by East Indians. Chinese restaurants were found on every island. How did these people end up in the Caribbean and the West Indies?

Crossing The Atlantic

We finally started the portion of the journey that I signed up for. We left Barbados 24 hours ago and have been sailing for more than 450 nautical miles. We are sailing at an average of 20 nautical miles per hour, and we are due to arrive in Funchal, Madeira Islands, Saturday morning. There's nothing but water all around. A little earlier, the *Reports from the Bridge* channel on my TV shows that the sea condition is rough, with waves between 7.5 and 12 feet high. It didn't feel bad at all. The pre-departure booklet says that if you feel your chair moving during meal time, hold on to the table. It hasn't happened yet.

Once in a while during the rough sailing, I felt that I was in a plane when the air was not smooth. Turbulence and the rough sea cause very similar sensations. Isn't that funny?

How Did I Get So Lucky?

I feel really lucky to have this opportunity to cross the Atlantic by sea. During the first few days, I asked myself often how I got to be so fortunate to have this experience. Then, while not staring at the sea and negotiating the steps, I had to devote more energy to keeping track of the meal times and locations, proper attire, and so on. The question of being so lucky doesn't come up as frequently anymore.

One of my favorite crew members is a young man from Indonesia. Well, the truth is that he mans the ice-cream counter and is always very pleasant and gives me double scoops without my asking. And I really like his name. On the crew name tags, all names are spelled in upper case and his name is DWI (pronounced *dwee*, not Dee Dubya Eye). Poor fellow. How can you not like him?

There's an internet café on board. It's a rather slow satellite connection. At 60 cents a minute, with a minimum charge of $6, the place is never full. At $36 an hour, I don't suppose many people are surfing for the sake of surfing. Also, it's amazing how quickly we learn to perceive that $12 an hour (ashore some of the islands) is an inexpensive way to connect to the Internet, and $6 an hour is a bargain not to be missed. Likewise, now that gas has gone over $2 a gallon in Texas for all grades, soon we will be thanking the gas companies for $1.99 per gallon! That is, if we will ever see that price again.

31. Transatlantic III: Life On Board

May 11, 2005 – Atlantic Ocean N26°45' W032°2'

The Sea Has Been Calm

This is our 4th day crossing the Atlantic. We are due to arrive in Funchal, Madeira Islands, in about 40 hours. The sea has been very calm today. In fact, you can row a boat across the big pond if the sea is this calm all the way. We are steadily heading northeast and the air temperature has been dropping. It is quite cool to be on the top deck early in the morning and late at night.

We thought the crossing would be a challenge for the people - to be confined aboard for so many days - but it has turned out fine. For myself, I definitely enjoy this part more than I do the island hopping.

Since the day after we left Barbados, we have been losing an hour every night. Since we kept the Eastern Daylight Saving time for a few days, sunrise has been as early as 5:30 am "ship time." There's no way I could wake myself up to see the sunrise. Now that we are catching up with the time change, sunrise this morning was at 7:35 am. It is awesome to see the sun coming up from the horizon, completely unobstructed. Sunsets have been equally awe-inspiring.

My Dinner Mates

My original assigned dinner mates didn't show up at the first dinner. The couple at the next table, Joe and Cathy from Urbana-Champaign, Illinois, invited me to join them for dessert and we have been sitting together ever since. They are an interesting couple. I don't remember how our conversation got to politics and religion at the second dinner. But we have them both covered and survived very well. Nothing is too taboo for our table anymore!

When I was in Bridgetown, Barbados, taking pictures of the ship at the dock, this nice Canadian lady, Myrna, asked me if I would like to be in the picture as well. She and her German Canadian husband, Guenter, are from Ottawa, Ontario. Their table mates disappeared before the first dinner was over, so they have been dining on their own for the first week. However, they have since joined our table. We had the same knowledgeable and multilingual waiter, Antonio from Napoli, Italy, so these changes weren't causing too much trouble. The waiter's assistant is from Montenegro and his name is Milan. He has a mischievous smile and reminds me of the school children from the Italian movie "Ciao Profesore." These four passengers have become the main people that I interact with. All four of them are retired or semi-retired, but we share one important common interest - life on board for the crew.

The American couple are staying in Italy for a week and the Canadians are staying for two and half weeks in Italy, Croatia, and Slovenia. During the 5-day crossing, the cruise offers 5 Italian classes for free. I went for the first two days and decided it was messing up my Spanish. My table mates have more incentive to learn the basics of the language.

A Professional Cruise Passenger

The first night of the cruise, the cruise director pointed out the gentleman who is crossing the Atlantic with MSC Cruises for the 6th time. I ran into Tom, of St. Catharines, Ontario, in one of the lounges. He is not retired, but somehow he manages to cruise a lot. He started taking cruises in 1988, and this is his 88th cruise. He has already booked an 11-day cruise to Tahiti in the south Pacific in July! He's a jolly fellow and introduced me to one of the performers, Holber. Holber is a magician from Colombia, currently residing in Italy when he is not at sea. Unfortunately I missed his show. He has two one-hour shows (first and second sitting) during the 18-day cruise, and maybe a 10-minute appearance at the end of the cruise. Nice job, eh?

TV, Radio, & Music

Supposedly the TV in the cabin has satellite reception. It doesn't work very well in the middle of the Atlantic as there simply is no need for satellite signals (per the cruise director), which is not a bad thing and I am not complaining. There's a channel that shows the safety procedures around the clock, rotating in the five major European languages. Then there is the channel that shows the navigational information and it's my favorite. One channel relays the images from the camera hooked to the front of the ship, and that's my "window" to the outside world. Great idea.

I am still trying to understand the logic behind what is available among the entertainment channels. In the West Indies and the Atlantic, we have Disney Kids (there are only 4 kids on the ship and 1 baby). Then there is Good Morning America (Charles Gibson and Diane Sawyer), but it only broadcasts the first hour of the show and repeats it the whole day. There is BET - Black Entertainment TV. Signals for these channels are not always reliable. In the middle of the night, we once had PBS, and that was very good. However, there are two channels that consistently have good reception - CBN (Christian Broadcast Network) and TBN (Trinity Broadcast Network). So, does that mean I am supposed to get my TV news from Pat Robertson at the 700 club? No way, Jose! Incidentally, have you seen the female anchor on CBN lately? Will someone please feed her? She makes Alley McBeal look overweight! Oh, one night, Robert Tilton, the ex-convict TV evangelist appeared on the screen and asked for money. Even though the TV was within easy reach from the bed, I didn't put my hand on the screen, as he requested, to feel the presence of God.

A supplement about TV - after we reached Funchal, we got many more decent channels, including TV stations out of Portugal, France, Germany, Spain, Italy and BBC World Service. No more propaganda disguised as news, as a discreet eye may detect in CBN. Again, my opinion. Definitely, no more TV preachers asking for my milk money!

There are three movie channels. This morning, I was watching Bruce Almighty (Jim Carey and Jennifer Anniston) in German, with Spanish subtitles. Sometimes the movies keep the English dialogs, with subtitles in French. More often, the dialogs have been dubbed in one language, and subtitled in another. If English or Spanish is not one of them, they have little use for me, really.

Again, I think these are done so that you are not tempted to stay in your cabin too much during the day. I noticed that if the passengers are in the cabin, and unless they are drinking from the mini bar, the ship is not making money. The people need to be out and about for the ship to sell more drinks, photo ops, shore excursions, and more chips for the casino.

While I was having lunch with Holber yesterday, we suddenly noticed that they were playing Celine Dion's "My Heart Will Go On," the theme song from Titanic, through the speakers in the cafeteria. And I heard it again this morning at breakfast. I always thought that the Titanic album was forever banned from cruise ships. It inevitably brings some very disturbing images to the mind while you are on board an ocean liner.

More About The Italian Lessons

During the crossing, the cruise offers 5 Italian lessons, among other interesting things, for the passengers who are visiting Italy. I have always heard if you speak one of the Roman languages (Italian, French, Spanish, Portuguese and Romanian), it is relatively easy to learn the others. While I have been surprised how much Italian I understand by using what I know about English and Spanish, I think the above claim only applies to people who speak one of these languages as their native tongue. I went to two of the Italian lessons and decided it was messing up my Spanish. After I learned the most important phrase "dove sono i gabinetti? *where's the bathroom*", I dropped the class. You really should learn how to ask this question in the local language wherever you go. When the need is urgent, and unless you don't mind miming it, you just have no time to look for an interpreter, you know!

Technically Speaking

There was a talk on the technical profile of the ship at the Broadway Theatre. It was fascinating to learn how things work. The ship is a little city of its own. It has oil refinery equipment to make maximum use of the fuel. Two thirds of the output from the generators goes to propel the ship, and one third is for lighting, heating, cooling, and what not. The ship generates enough power for a city of 8,000 to 10,000 people. Drinking water is distilled on board and water to wash comes from the desalinating plants on the lower deck. The ship is fully stabilized, with the help of two underwater wings of 9 square meters each, so the rolling of the ship is kept to a minimum, but pitching cannot be helped. The navigation controls are fully integrated with the GPS system to eliminate human calculation error.

During the talk, one passenger asked the cruise director if anyone had ever fallen into the water from the ship. The director relayed this story. In his 16 years of cruise experience, the "Man Over Board" alarm went off only once. It was in Mykonos, Greece. The ship was docked and was about to leave port when the "Man Over Board" alarm was sounded. A lifeboat was launched to save the man, who fought the rescue team and refused to get into the boat, assumedly in shock from the trauma. The team eventually managed to get him back on the ship and dried him off with the awaiting towels; that's when they realized that the man was just taking a swim in the nearby water and he wasn't a passenger of the ship after all.

32. Transatlantic IV: Upstairs Downstairs

May 13, 2005 – Atlantic Ocean N30°41.466' W021°23.578'

On the ship, food is readily available and not bad at all, and entertainment is plentiful. The ship is only two-years old and it's very nice. However, the things that interest me the most are the ocean and the life aboard for the crew. Two weeks into the trip, my conclusion is that this is a real life Upstairs Downstairs (the BBC TV program). And physically, we are positioned that way as well.

Crew Life

I collected these stories on board the ship. Most of them I heard from fellow passengers who have many more experiences traveling on cruise ships than I have. They could be stories that apply to most liners. Others I asked the crew members about directly, such as stories about working hours and scheduling. There is no way I can verify them, nor do I intend to. So, again, read this as if you are reading the National Inquirer! I am not repeating them as facts, but as "stories I have heard." Some are merely my opinions, and I have plenty!

First of all, this cruise ship lifestyle is a fantasy. How often do you have smoked salmon for breakfast? 18 days in a row? Where else on earth do you have people catering to your every wish from sunrise till after midnight? My table mates and I share the same curiosity. So, we talked to our respective sources throughout the day and compared notes at dinner.

The Many Nationalities Of The Crew

First of all, I want to make it clear that the service on board has been generally very good. The five of us at the dinner table are unanimous about it. Having said that, I find that the service you get from any crew members has a lot to do with their nationality. I am risking overgeneralization here, but it seems that the poorer the country of origin, the more cheerful one appears. Hence, we mostly get heart-warming smiles from both the Indonesians (they work in the cafeteria, at the ice cream stand, and at the midnight buffet) and the folks from Madagascar (most of them work in the housekeeping department). The Croatians and Romanians are found in the housekeeping department, and some, along with the Bulgarians and Hungarians, are in the Casino, the lounges, the restaurants, and the bars. The folks who work in the Entertainment department are western Europeans, most of them Italian polyglots. Then there are the performers. There is a team of flamenco dancers who are Spaniards. The other dancers, singers, and musicians are from all over Europe. There are also 25 Peruvians, working in various departments.

The waiters are mostly Italians. The bus boys can be any of the others, as well as some Italians. In spite of the fact that this is an Italian liner, the official language onboard is English, which means that one must speak English to get a job there, though knowing Italian would be, as you can imagine, extremely helpful, as your boss is very likely to be Italian. Therefore, everyone has a working command over the English language. Of course, the waiters and the entertainers speak a minimum of three languages, often four, and sometimes five. Our waiter is from Napoli, Italy, and his assistant is from Montenegro (south of Croatia, west of Yugoslavia, in case you wonder). They both speak multiple languages.

Not everyone works for the cruise company. The performers are subcontracted. The same is also true for the people in the gymnasium, the photographers, and the salespersons in the stores. We decided it was too difficult to draw a clear line between employees and subcontractors.

Working Hours

When I first learned that some of these people have been working non-stop since the end of November, I was rather shocked. There is no such thing as Sunday. They work between 8 to 10 hours a day, seven days a week, until they get off the ship at the end of their contract. It seems like most people work 9-10 months in a row and then have a vacation back home for 2-3 months consecutively. I thought it was rather tough. But when I spoke to a young man from Romania, he said most of his friends also work in the industry, so it doesn't bother him that much. Besides, when he's off during those 2-3 months, he throws away his watch and keeps no schedule whatsoever. And to do that, we would have to take a mini sabbatical. He also said that it's not like his work demands physical energy or brain work.

I used to complain how the weekly travel requirement of my job causes me to have a social life calendar the size of a piece of toilet paper, but now I have seen what others endure, and I shall complain no more. At least I get to sleep in my own bed every weekend and my friends can call me on the cell phone, should they care to do so.

Contract & Compensation

Cruise ship hiring is mostly done through agencies. I heard that the agency will send you to cruise ship schools to learn the trade and the specialization, and then you are certified if you meet all the standards. However, most people already have hotel and/or restaurant experience before they enter this line of work. Nonetheless, the certification process, along with the first year contract, costs US$2,000 in Asia and Latin America; subsequent yearly contracts cost $1,000 apiece. So, you literally pay to work. And some jobs on board carry a monthly salary tag of $500. We will keep that in mind when we do our tipping at the end of the trip. Incidentally, I heard that in the late eighties and early nineties, some of the crew members on the American liners were paid $50 a month. And the rest is entirely the result of tipping.

I was initially shocked, and then didn't quite know what to think, when I learned that one's salary on board a ship varies based on one's country of origin, even though one might be doing exactly the same job as someone from another country. The rationale behind this disparity is that they have to do this to attract the more skilled labor from countries that have a higher cost of living. It does make sense intellectually, but I wouldn't be the least bit surprised if the crew members from the less expensive countries feel short-changed by this logic. I do, at a practical level, realize that nobody puts a gun to their heads to join the ship. They are not in slavery, even though the hours might suggest otherwise. They all do so voluntarily and they do it because it's one step (or several) above where they were before boarding the ship. Or they want to avoid their spouses and children at home. Or they want to see the world (at least a little bit of it). Or this is the best option at their disposal at this point.

At any rate, comparing one's salary with one's peers is never a good idea. What do you do with the information anyway? Do you laugh or cry depending on the difference?

Food & Beverages

I fully expected that the food downstairs is nothing like the food upstairs, and I would be out of my mind if I should expect otherwise. I can also imagine that the large amount of leftovers become the meal for the crew the next day, supplemented with rice and spaghetti. And some people just get tired of pizza and spaghetti after a few months. That certainly explains why they are so trim in general. There's a bar for the crew on the lower deck and beer is available at a reduced rate, sometimes as cheap as 50 cents a glass. This is true for all cruise ships. You can easily drink your dinner that way.

The internet is also available for the crew, at a reduced rate, but still very high compared with what one pays at home. So, one just makes friends on the ship. Unless they are officers, they have to share their cabins with someone else.

This life really requires some special personality to handle it. Some obviously enjoy it or they wouldn't stay in this line of work for 16 years. For myself, if I were to be without the internet and the social life that I am accustomed to, however small my social calendar tends to be, the "Man Over Board" alarm would sound soon enough. And please do not bother to lower the lifeboat.

33. Transatlantic V: Funchal - Paradise Discovered

May 15, 2005 – Atlantic Ocean N34°58.45' W009°14.88'

"We Almost Made It!"

The day before we reached Funchal, the cruise director came on the speaker from the bridge, as he did every day, in 5 languages fluently, to keep us passengers informed of the progress of the crossing. He started by quoting the distance we had traveled since leaving Barbados, the previous port of call, and the distance left for Funchal. Then he said, "we almost made it." It was Friday 13th.

The English-speaking passengers all stopped eating and digested the sentence instead. We quickly realized that what he meant to say was "we've almost made it" or "we are almost there." He seemed to have translated the idea from Italian to English. This is a little slip of translation, but it made quite a big difference in meaning and created a comical scenario. We had a good chuckle. Mind you, this man speaks five languages fluently while he's half asleep, and his English is nearly perfect. I am mentioning this because, first, it was funny (not haha funny, but funny), and because, second, I want to take this opportunity to point out that English is more difficult to master than most native speakers realize. After 36 years of learning and using it, I still harbor doubts with respect to many areas of the language.

Funchal, Madeira Islands

While this is one of the most popular vacation spots for Europeans, I would imagine this is unfamiliar territory for most of my North American and Asian friends. There is simply no easy way to get here from the North American continent. I certainly didn't know much about the Madeira Islands until yesterday.

The Madeira Islands were discovered and colonized by the Portuguese. The captain involved was supposed to go to Africa to strengthen the Portuguese interests in its colonies there, but the drift of the ocean took his ship to the Madeira Islands instead. In other words, they were lost, really. The rest was history.

It's located off the Moroccan coast and (very) roughly 500 nautical miles from the Strait of Gibraltar. The island has a population of 250,000, 99.9% of whom are Portuguese descendants. I saw two black people at one of the bus stops. Also I saw a Chinese restaurant, so I imagine there are a couple of Chinese people here, possibly from Macau.

This island is beautiful, charming, quaint, clean, safe, and friendly. Honestly, any pleasant and positive adjective will apply. There must be a really strict zoning law as almost all the houses have red rooftops. Funchal is the capital of the island and the vast majority of the people live here. This is a popular port of call for the European cruises that venture out of the Mediterranean and there is a plethora of scheduled and charter flights from Europe. Even though tourism is vital to the island's economy, the people are not pushy about it at all. It was a refreshing contrast from most popular vacation spots.

The Island Of Flowers

There is quite a culture of flowers on this island. A fellow solo traveler invited me to hike one of the some 50 trails. We took the bus to the top of the mountain. Up on the top of the mountain, we saw some of the simpler homes (still plenty charming). However, they all have an unobstructed and unbeatable view of the city and the endless ocean. That view alone is worth a few million dollars in Hong Kong. All the homes have beautifully decorated entry ways. I saw a little corner of the Botanical Garden and it was breathtaking.

The streets are lined with trees that have flowers on them. There are flowers everywhere you look. The flower market features flowers that I can neither name nor describe in terms of the colors! Aside from Switzerland and Denmark, this is the most organized place I have seen. Switzerland has the mountain but lacks the ocean. Denmark has the ocean but the tallest hill is merely 500 feet tall. In that sense, this place might have them beat in terms of natural beauty.

All the passengers couldn't stop talking about the island after we returned to the ship. The word "paradise" was used often at the dinner table to describe the Madeira Islands.

I will definitely return to this island in the future to savor her beauty; however, I would like to spend at least a week here. Since this place is rather removed from continental Europe, most people who don't have to deal with tourists speak limited English. I recommend a basic course in Portuguese before one arrives to spend a week or more here. Learning the basic greetings will take you a long way. The only Portuguese word I could think of was "obligato" (thank you) and even that brought a few smiles. If nothing else, learn how to say "where's the bathroom?" It will pay off. Or you will be helping to "water" their trees.

34. Transatlantic VI: Mediterranean Ports Of Call

May 18, 2005 – Barcelona, Spain

Going Through The Strait Of Gibraltar

We officially left the Atlantic Ocean when we entered the Mediterranean Sea through the Strait of Gibraltar. That was the day when the cruise started to wind down and we had our last formal evening and the Captain's farewell cocktail party (free drinks again), and we said thanks and farewell to the performers, chefs and officers on board. It was midnight when we entered the Strait. However, the sky was clear enough and we were able to see both Europe (Spain) and Africa (Morocco) at the same time. It was a thrilling experience. It was also the first time I felt that the cruise has been long enough and I was ready to leave the ship, but I certainly can be talked into being pampered for three more days.

Malaga

Our first port of call in the Mediterranean was Malaga, the capital of Andalusia, in southern Spain. It is a beautiful city, but after Funchal, it takes a lot more to excite the senses of beauty. The Canadian couple, Myrna and Guenter, and I went to the Tourist Information office in town and the gentleman behind the desk recommended Nerja, Costa del Sol, a coast town. The bus ride took more than an hour.

Southern Spain is to Europeans like Florida is to north Americans. This is obvious when the real estate development signs are in English first, then Spanish. Nerja is actually quaint. It features lots of hotels and there is a series of intimate beaches, popular among the sun worshippers.

Siesta Time

We returned to Malaga right after 2:00 in the afternoon and split up to do our own sightseeing here. I was hoping to find a phone card and an internet cafe, and then get some sightseeing in before returning to the ship. Well, most of the shops closed between two and five in the afternoon. Siesta time! It was quite an inconvenience for those like me who only have a few hours in the city. I ended up not accomplishing either task. The cathedral in the city is a gorgeous building and I started to play with my camera to take pictures inside the church. The knowledge proved to be handy the next evening in Barcelona. After walking for more than 12 miles, I returned to the ship just before the afternoon ice-cream stand shut down.

We sailed for Barcelona. To my surprise and delight, the Mediterranean was rougher than the Atlantic. And we had a beautiful sunset on this day.

A Word About The Canadian Fellow Travelers

When I was in Barbados, I was taking pictures of the ship when Myrna kindly volunteered to take picture of me with the ship. She and her husband Guenter have been married for 37 years. I have seen newlyweds who are less in love (specifically, on an overnight train from Barcelona to Paris a few years ago!) We ended up spending a lot of time together for the rest of the cruise. Their assigned table was only two tables behind me at the dining restaurant, but I never saw them because I sat facing the ocean. Their table mates left them in the middle of the first dinner, reasons unknown, and when I introduced them to my table mates, we invited them to join our table. They were very friendly and they didn't smell (I was still thinking why their table mates left mid-dinner), so I figured it was safe to have them join us. It was nice to have more people to dine with during the 5-day crossing. The arrangement turned out to be most pleasing for all involved.

Myrna and Guenter can be poster kids for Rick Steves, the well known backpack travel expert. They did their homework as to what to see in each port. I offered them the bait of free translation in Spain if they allowed me to tag along. It worked out perfectly well for both parties. They are definitely travelers instead of tourists. After the cruise, they are staying in Europe to visit Slovenia and Croatia for more than two weeks, each taking only a backpack weighing no more than 15-18 pounds each for the two weeks. My shaving kit weighs half that much! They taught me a lot about traveling and I am determined to travel lighter in the future.

Barcelona

The tail wind that caused the sea to be rough pushed us into the port of Barcelona two and half hours ahead of schedule. This was the only port where we had an overnight stay. Like Sydney in Australia, I enjoyed my second visit to Barcelona much more so than my first. We disembarked after dinner and walked to the Poble Espanya (*Spanish Village*, it's in Catalan). Barcelona is the second largest city in Spain. And it's very well organized. This is one of the major compounds for the Olympic Games and it features Spanish architecture throughout the country. The place is open to visitors until two in the morning. We got there after 9 pm and almost had the place all to ourselves, other than those who went there for the restaurants and bars. We returned to the ship just in time for the midnight buffet.

Gaudi's Barcelona

The next morning we met for breakfast before seven and headed out again to take advantage of the port time. The Sagrada Familia (Holy Family) Cathedral designed by Gaudi has been under construction since 1882. It was our first stop. The pictures on my website will do more justice than my words.

When we got back to the ship, we heard that two gentlemen were mugged in town. One 85 year-old man joined one of the shore excursions and the tour group lost him at a church. It turned out that the gang, who were reportedly Gypsies, sprayed something on his leg, and proceeded to apologize and cleaned it up. Meanwhile, they managed to take his wallet out of his back pocket, took out the cash, and returned the wallet to his pocket. So, he only lost cash, but not his credit cards and other IDs. If they must mug someone, I actually wouldn't be too mad if they had the decency to allow me to keep my credit cards, passports and IDs. Well, after they finished cleaning up (and out) the victim, the gentleman patted his pocket and found that his wallet was still there, so he didn't think much of it. Unable to find the now lost tour member, the tour group had left the church by then as the gangway was soon closing at that point. The gentleman took a taxi back to the ship, and only when he opened his wallet did he realize what had transpired earlier. Moral of the lesson: gentlemen, please don't put your wallet in your back pocket when you travel in the big cities of Europe in general, or you will run the risk of ending up in a similar story!

35. Transatlantic VII: Conclusion

May 19, 2005 – 36,000 Feet above the Atlantic

Time Change On Board

During the Atlantic crossing, the ship clock moved forward an hour each night. This is much better than moving the clock six hours ahead in one shot, as one would do traveling by air.

You would think that one hour a day is an easy adjustment. Not so, if you go to the midnight buffet religiously like I did. Each night after the buffet, I went to entertain myself, and sometimes the cleaning crew, at one of the piano bars by playing what I could remember off the top of my head. I couldn't play the piano, nor should they have allowed me, while there were passengers and professional musicians around. Some passengers did play in the lounge during the day when there were no professional musicians at work, but they were very good. As a result, I normally didn't get to sleep until 3 or 4 am, with the clock already moved forward one hour at 2 am. Even on board the ship, they didn't want to cut into the bar closing time by effecting the time change too early. One morning, afternoon rather, I slept so late that I missed the 6:30 am-10 am breakfast, the 10 am-noon croissant service, and the noon-2 pm lunch. I woke up to the 2 pm-5 pm ice-cream and pizza service. That was a bit excessive, but totally indulgent, I must say.

The End Of The Journey

We left Barcelona at noon and sailed overnight to the final destination of the journey - Genoa, Italy, and arrived this morning at eight. The non-Schengen nationalities were requested to collect their passports in the Broadway Theatre.

The Schengen Agreement

From what I understand, basically, it is an agreement signed by a group of countries inside the now European Union *(Spain, France, Italy and Portugal are the ones I visited on this trip, but there are more though)*. For foreigners, the important implication of this agreement is that you only need to get a tourist visa from the country of port of entry (air, sea, or land) and that visa is good for all the participating countries in the agreement. Since the United States has an agreement with the European Union, Americans are allowed to travel in the EU member countries without a visa. A passport is, of course, still required, but that doesn't mean you don't have to clear immigration and customs. Now that the European Union is in full force, the concept of the Schengen Agreement may seem more confusing now than ever before for Americans because it doesn't apply to us anymore. Some countries may have an agreement with the Schengen countries, but not with the European Union. And that's why the term is still very much relevant, in case you wonder. The Europeans on the cruise already returned to Europe officially after the Madeira Islands and, in spirit, their immigration clearing took place there. The cruise ship keeps the passports for the non EU passengers and we officially clear immigration in Genoa. And I have a stamp in my passport to prove that.

Incidentally, if you know that the above is not a true account of the Schengen Agreement, I would like to be informed.

Back To Reality

Everyone was generally civil and pleasant during the 18-day cruise, except the few passengers who were determined to make asses of themselves (excuse the language, but there's no close substitute here) during the journey, making everyone serving them work doubly as hard to earn their salaries. But the ugliness of human nature showed its face during the less than ideal arrangement of passport distribution. And at that exact moment, I realized that the fantasy of cruise lifestyle was over. We had successfully and seamlessly returned to reality.

During the transfer to the airport, the two ladies behind me complained about how disorganized the Italians were and that they would never take an Italian cruise again. They were specifically dismayed that the cruise didn't give them enough time to do shopping in the ports of call. Obviously, they missed the point that this is a repositioning cruise. Still, there was plenty of time for shopping in the ports of call if one so desired. The one thing they clearly didn't complain about was that the cruise cost them as little as $1,000 a person for the crossing, assuming they were sharing a cabin. The staff on board may now take a collective sigh of relief knowing that these people are not returning to haunt them in the future. These two are, incidentally, Americans. Am I being unpatriotic by naming their nationality in public in this light? In this post 9-11 environment, I am afraid I am.

The Italian lady on the bus explained that it would cost one Euro to get a luggage cart at the airport. These two ladies behind me exclaimed, "Who would have a Euro?!" Helloooooo? We were using them as early as Martinique 13 days earlier, and had been using them since the Madeira Islands. I was too tired to be polite and not tired enough to keep my mouth shut, so I turned to my fellow countrywomen and said in a plain and tired voice, "We are not in America anymore. We haven't been since we left St. Thomas, fourteen days ago." They said nothing else in my presence.

A Final Word About Cruise

It is definitely a much more interesting way to cross the pond by sea than by air. It was my first cruise, so I have nothing to compare it with, though I know that it won't be easy to top this experience. A 7-day Caribbean cruise sounds just too short! I had enjoyed it as much as I thought I would. Seeing the ocean for such an extended period of time reminded me of how small and insignificant the human race is in the big scheme of things. I should be less affected by the mundane things in life. It would be nicer if I had even more time to meditate during the trip, but I couldn't resist the temptation of all the food and fruit. Having said this, I don't think I will become addicted to this type of travel. It's fun to do it once in a (long) while, but to do it all the time can be mind-numbing as this is definitely a very artificial reality as far as I can see. The cruise ship fills your hours with activities, and it can easily be interpreted as having a life. And I believe that having a full calendar does not necessarily translate into a full life.

Oh, by the way, I did keep my resolution of not using the elevator during the whole trip, until I disembarked with the luggage. And, more surprisingly, I didn't place a single bet in the casino. Not too bad for a Chinese person who thinks he knows how blackjack should be played!

However, if you have 20 days to spare, and you want to be away from phones and e-mails (unless you are willing to pay $36 for an hour), this can be a most fascinating experience. I recommend it. I am still interested in a freighter some time in the future.

Back To Dallas, Then Costa Rica

I will be in Dallas for the weekend - to do laundry for the last three weeks, put away the formal attire, see the doctor one more time to check on my case of tendonitis, and then I am flying back to Costa Rica on Sunday afternoon to fulfill my commitment with the church.

I just realized that I have given a lot of coverage to the transatlantic crossing, but I think the fact that I have more time on my hands has something to do with it, in addition to experiencing all these new things. Thanks for your interest.

36. Last Leg In Costa Rica

May 27, 2005 – San Jose, Costa Rica

Returning To Costa Rica

My body came back to Costa Rica last Sunday (May 22); my mind arrived two days later. The previous week turned out to be rather crazy. The whirlwind days in Spain, the jet lag, and the hectic weekend in Dallas had me drained when I finally got to slow down. I woke up Monday morning to the utmost disorientation and spent almost half an hour in bed trying to figure out where I was, alternating between being awake and being asleep. My intention was to go to work on Monday, but I spent the whole day at home to recoup instead, and to work on the website.

In-flight Entertainment?

When I flew back from Dallas to Costa Rica in February and from Costa Rica to Dallas earlier in late April, I happened to sit next to a Mennonite both times. So, I wasn't sure if I would run into a third one in a row on this flight. They were both interesting people to talk to. The last one I met, Seth of Salt Lake City, shared with me a lot about his work and family. He has an interesting story. He was on a mission trip to Columbia, promoting books for home schooling families! His parents moved to Bolivia as missionaries when he was 9 or 10 and they stayed there until he was an adult. He went through school with the local kids and speaks fluent Spanish. He met his American wife in Bolivia, as she was there in school for the same reason.

They are married with 6 kids, and more is definitely possible. He showed me pictures of his family and they look like reformed Amish people. Well, they use computers as he has a home-based billing service for medical doctors. We talked nonstop from Miami to Dallas. When he asked me about my religious beliefs, I told him that I don't like talking about religion because I am not good at talking about it. We did anyway. It was very interesting, to say the least. I was surprised that, as religious as he seemed to be, he thought it was a good thing that the US military is in Iraq. I obviously mistook that his seemingly more pure form of religion would be free of political influence. I was wrong. I was tempted to ask him how his "God" might feel about Iraqi collateral damage, but I decided to pick my battle elsewhere. And I didn't have to wait long.

At one point, he mentioned that his family doesn't watch TV at home because there's nothing on that's worthwhile to watch. I disagreed as I have learned quite a few things from PBS, A&E, the History channel, etc. (And thanks to Golden Girls for a touch of sense of humor.) He believes that even though you can sometimes find something edible from the trash (i.e., TV media), trash is still trash. I contested and said that most television programs were trash because he compared them to trash. For the sake of argument, I compared them to a refrigerator. Even though some food was spoiled, that didn't mean we should throw good food out with the bad food. He learned that a small Asian man could be feisty verbally. We moved on to the next topic quickly; education it was, I believe. The truth of the matter is that I had previously made a resolution to watch less TV once I returned to the US. I really waste too much time on that box. In the end, he gave me his business card and invited me to Salt Lake City to meet his family in case I ever want to go and visit. Someday maybe, but I am not counting on it.

Last Leg In Central America

Now that everybody knows I am leaving Costa Rica for good by the end June, things have started to get busy. Well, they had always known, but the sense of urgency was not there until I told them that I had started the countdown.

The unconscious computer networking project got revived this week. And I had a meeting with the administrator and a new guy on the team this Wednesday to catch him up on the happenings. He's a member of the church and offered to help the project by donating his time and his resources - contract rates, much needed expertise, and what-not. In fact, what we really needed was $18,000 and a half time network administrator. The meeting was at 7:30 in the morning. It's public knowledge that I am not a morning person. It's by all means too early to talk about hardware networking at this ungodly hour. Definitely not in Spanish. To make things worse, the new guy has somewhat of a lisp. It really distorted a lot of sounds. We survived. Fortunately, I had an idea of what was going on, but I was very quiet for the whole hour.

On a related note, before I left Costa Rica in late April, I had been evaluating software that was donated to the church/school. Actually, I was learning to use the software so that I could teach the folks at the church/school how to use it. The user-guide was practically nonexistent. I gave them a list of my findings and my questions. It wasn't my intention, but I accidentally talked them out of that locally developed software. To put it mildly, that thing leaves a lot to be desired! The folks at the church/school are finally convinced that certain things shouldn't be free! It took me three months to get that message across. So, I am now evaluating software packages again, but this time it will be quicker, and possibly easier, as time is running out! If they want my input to be part of the decision, they have to make it happen now. As an Oracle practitioner, I am a bit embarrassed to say that I am pushing Quick Books and Peachtree these days! The price is right, and the functions are there! It's the right move for them. Stay tuned.

And then there are more English classes scheduled for the month. A good friend of mine is coming to visit for the week of June 6, so I will play tourist and interpreter again for a week. And I will be going to do some other community work with yet another organization, maybe two days a week. Then I was invited to help out with a children's day camp at another church. Jenifer (this is correct spelling) is a missionary from Denver and she works in two churches. So I see her twice every week at my church. She is the organizer of the camp and it is scheduled this Saturday. Yahoo! I finally get to work with children, about which I have a lot to say. But I will wait until the camp is over.

All this last-minute increased workload reminds me of one peculiar human behavior: we sometimes don't value people in our lives until they are gone or they are in their death beds. That's how I feel now. If this keeps up, I will probably get more accomplished in these last six weeks than in the previous five months combined!

Supplement On Schengen Agreement

After reading the previous journal entry, Melanie, a German friend of mine who resides in Holland, sent me an e-mail to further clarify the Schengen Agreement. She said:

"To us, the Schengen agreement means that we can travel to and from Schengen countries just as you travel between US states. For example, we don't have to stop anymore when we cross the border to Belgium or Germany by car. There is no more passport control or custom. Just a sign that says 'Welcome to....'"

Thanks Mel. That explains why every time I enter and exit the UK within the EU (except from and to the Republic of Ireland), I have to go through immigration and customs control. UK didn't sign the Schengen Agreement.

37. Children's Day Camp

May 29, 2005 - San Jose, Costa Rica

My friend Jenifer invited me to help her with the children's day camp today at her other church in Pavas, a suburb of San Jose. I turned down a weekend trip to Guanacaste on the Pacific Coast to join the camp. It was all worth it. The US Embassy is also located in Pavas, but it's on the good side. The other side of Pavas is arguably one of the poorest neighborhoods in the central valley. Hence, foreigners normally don't go there, especially after dark and on their own.

How Do You Plan With Latinos?

I am going to get a lot of gripes just for this heading.

The church - Ministries of Victory - occupies a unit in a small strip mall owned by a Taiwanese man. The kids in the church signed up and they could register a friend as well. Forty-five kids in total signed up. On the day of the event, we ended up having seventy-five kids. Half of the ones who registered didn't show. There were more "unregistered" names than there were registered ones. How do you plan lunch and dinner when people have no respect for this registration process? A friend told me that in one of her cousin's wedding, some extra fifty people showed up that didn't bother to RSVP. It was a sit-down dinner! This same attitude permeates among my Hispanic friends in Texas as well. They definitely have a much more relaxed attitude toward this area of social life.

The Kids

The kids were all very excited about the day camp - it's the first for the church. Some of the kids come from rather poor families. I heard that one kid comes from a household of five and sometimes the family's weekly budget for food is slightly more than $10. You can safely bet that rice, beans and sugar, and maybe coffee are all they can afford. You are lucky if you are not hungry, so you can forget about nutrition.

Because of the fact that I am Chinese, the kids seemed very interested in talking to me, which was very surprising to me. There were more Chinese restaurants in that area than I could count. It might be because I was one whom they could approach and ask questions. Well, the fact that I had a camera in my hand helped, I am sure. One little girl was especially curious and asked me a lot about Hong Kong and Texas. We had a lovely chat. Then she asked me, "cómo es tu himno nacional?" Since the "h" has no sound in Spanish, I didn't associate the "imno" sound with "hymn." She asked three times and I still didn't get it. The little boy who has been sitting in quietly on our conversation lost his patience and screamed the question at a slower speed, repeating the very exact words. I finally understood "what's your national anthem like," and I turned to him with a gentle smile, saying "*chico, soy solo tonto, no soy sordo*" or "kid, I am only stupid, I am not deaf." Too bad he was too young to get the humor. However, I was glad to find that non-Americans also raise their voices and slow their speech in an attempt to improve communication with foreigners! He was an eight year-old kid! And it worked for him. Looking back, this might have been a horrible reinforcement for him. He's going to think that foreigners will understand him if he slows down his speech and raises his voice.

I was rather distraught when I found out that the kids lied to me, more than once, when I was handing out lunch and dinner. They lied in order to get a second plate. Jenifer told me that this is just their basic survival skills. That still didn't sit well with me. And in my mind, I couldn't stop comparing them with the kids I met in the orphanage in the Dominican Republic. Those kids were also very poor but behaved like angels. Now, I must ask myself what accounts for the difference in behavior.

Oh, I found out that I really don't like it when a child addresses me as "chino." That sounds extra disrespectful coming from a child. I feel okay, though, when they call me "chinito" or "little Chinese," because it sounds friendly. Whenever the kids called me chino, I always told them that 'my name is Andy'. They seemed to get the message.

The Games

The games chosen (designed) by Jenifer had me on edge all day. I thought for sure that someone was going to get injured badly. Without boring you with the details here, let's just say that any of the games could be heaven for ambulance chasers, if they took place in the States. I decided that if any of the kids had contagious and fatal diseases, we could have started an epidemic. But then I forgot that their immune systems are much stronger simply because they grew up in that environment.

The kids seemed to have thoroughly enjoyed the games, which reminded me once again how little I know about children. If I were to design the games, no doubt, it would resemble a junior Jeopardy tournament! Nobody would get hurt as long as they didn't get too excited with their thumbs on the buzzers.

The Biblical Lesson

It's a church sponsored activity, so you bet there would be a biblical lesson in the program. Jenifer delivered the lesson. It didn't matter if I agreed with the lesson. That's not my point. However, during the lesson, it dawned on me that you can have the kids' undivided attention for 20 minutes or so by giving them a few games, a hot dog, a movie, a sandwich, and a sugar drink. That's about the cheapest advertisement you can find on earth. And if you are out to evangelize the world, starting with the kids might be your best bet yet.

Since kids are, by nature, impressionable and they want to please the adults, I have started to wonder what brands of Christianity are being spread around the world using this very method. If the message is extreme, it can definitely do more harm than good in the long run for the child, and for the world as well.

38. A Walk In The Wild - Part I

May 31, 2005 – San Jose, Costa Rica

My Costa Rica

Whenever people find out that I have been living in Costa Rica since Thanksgiving, they usually comment how beautiful the country is. Well, the country is undeniably beautiful, if you go do the tourist things in the rainforest, the volcanoes, the beaches, and so on. But that's not the Costa Rica in which I live. Mine is more of a local version which the tourism board will do all that is possible to shield you from.

Florie, my receptionist friend, introduced me to a group of people called Renacer, or Rebirth. This group works under the umbrella of Cristo para la Ciudad, or Christ for the City. Let me take this opportunity to point out that even though I call myself a Christian, it matters not if the organization is Buddhist or of any other religion or even agnosticism; I would be glad to be part of it as long as the religious followers do their work in a manner that is in line with my value system. Here in Costa Rica, you can safely bet that most organizations tend to have a Christian flavor to them. Catholicism is the national religion after all.

Getting Into A Volkswagen Van With Strangers

Ronald from Rebirth and I finally got connected and he and his group were to pick me up at Sabanilla Park at 8:00 Tuesday morning. I trusted Florie, and so I trusted Ronald. I was to look for a white Volkswagen Van.

When the van pulled up, I smiled. I really wanted to ask them, "Where's the peace logo?" This is the kind of van that was popular in the 70s and 80s, among the free souls, before Chrysler came up with the Minivan. On TV, I have seldom seen one of those without a peace logo on it. I got in the van and realized I was among total strangers - 3 men, and not knowing where I was going. They could have easily sold me into slavery should they think I could be worth anything. We drove around the city in different neighborhoods and picked up 3 more women, one of them being the pastor of the group, before heading for Guarari. Guarari is a subsection in the city of Heredia, the city north of San Jose, about 40 minutes and a world away.

The Work

This group of people chooses to work with the most disadvantaged and even those abandoned by the society. They run a children's club on Tuesday morning for the younger ones and on Tuesday in the afternoon for those in their early teens. I met the kids in the morning and was introduced to them. These children have no place to go play that's safe. Ronald explained to me the needs of the group and he said they needed psychological care most of all, followed by medical and dental care. A female doctor used to come on Fridays to give them free medical attention but she no longer could do it.

As an example, a 9 year-old boy was pointed out to me. Other than his worn-out clothes, he looked "normal" on the surface. The kid, however, is a victim of sexual abuse by a group of teenagers. His mother works as a prostitute so he has no father that he knows of. His grandmother, the only source of stability in his life, is dying of cancer. The boy doesn't go to school and he needs mental health attention. Still at a single digit age, he has been through more suffering than most adults in the first world.

One 12 year-old girl that I met was regularly providing sexual favors a year ago, in exchange for bread, not even money. Not that the situation would have been any more acceptable if cash was involved in the transaction. What I am trying to point out is that some bad people are really taking advantage of these poor kids. Since I have laid out some rather personal specifics regarding these two kids, I have made sure to exclude them in the photos in the Galleries section on the website. When you see the pictures on the website that go along with this story, don't look for these two as they will not be included. That's the least I can do to protect them.

A Walk In The Wild

After lunch, I was taken to see the neighborhood, what they called the Zona Roja (Red Zone). This place is about as dangerous as it gets in the country. Ronald and Giovanni drove the van to the Red Zone, about two blocks away from the children's center, and parked it in front of a hair salon. We left our backpacks back in the church. I had my camera with me (I have learned not to go anywhere without it), and they told me to pull my T-shirt out of my jeans so that it would cover the camera case. We proceeded through the main "street".

We brought a sack of individually packed snacks to hand out to the folks. As soon as we started our walk, I realized that this was the ugliest of humanity I have ever seen with my own eyes. And up close. These people would be the lepers in the biblical days. There was a man sitting in each corner of the passage ways - calling them "streets" would be a major misnomer.

I was told that if I were to enter here by myself (don't worry, I am not that crazy), there's absolutely no doubt that I would be robbed, assaulted, and maybe even fatally injured. It took this ministry many years to establish the trust with the people for them to be allowed here. The signs of drug addiction were everywhere. Prostitution seems to always go hand-in-hand with drugs. Being in the very middle of the slum physically was rather overwhelming emotionally. I remember thinking that when one loses all his human dignity, it's about as sad as it can get. The body becomes nothing but a tool to get the next fix. The ironic vicious cycle is that they spend the money on further destroying their bodies, the only means of income that they know of. Not everyone can find a market for their bodies; when this happens, one naturally resorts to stealing and robbing. Addiction is a horrible thing. Addiction of any kind.

I was surprised to see that there were two or three "pulperias," or corner stores, inside the slum. The place is not paved; one could imagine that inside most of the homes the floor is just dirt. There is a tradition of shaking hands among men in this country, even among total strangers. If someone offers you his hand, and you don't reciprocate, it is a major insult. Since I was with people that were known to the neighborhood, hands were extended towards me as well. I shook their hands and gently exchanged niceties with them. I was told not to run no matter what. A running stranger can cause some serious consequences in this place. Reality is so much more forceful than what one sees behind a TV screen.

What shocked me was that there was a noticeable population of babies and children living here. There is a coffee plantation across the paved main street, and the homeless sleep there on cardboard and whatever they can find. This is the tropics and when it rains here, it literally pours. They told me that some of the children are in the homeless category.

Ronald knew that I wanted to take some pictures and he found a safe spot for me to do so. And I also sneaked a few shots myself behind his back. I was glad that I bought a really small camera. It would be too difficult to lug along a camera any bigger without being noticed.

39. A Walk In The Wild - Part II

May 31, 2005 – San Jose, Costa Rica

Double Whammy For Women

There are rehabilitation centers for drug addicts in this country. However, they are mostly private and are prohibitively expensive for the addicts. Another thing is that most of the centers cater exclusively to men. For a woman addict, this is truly a double whammy.

Ronald told me that there was a 20 year-old woman who asked the Renacer group for help to put her in a rehabilitation center. These are truly the only people one can help. If they are not willing to help themselves, then any effort will be futile. We looked for that woman, but we couldn't find her.

The Feeding Hand Got Bitten

When we were walking back to the car, I thought to myself how amazing it was that these two men had earned the trust of the locals and that the van was still there as we left it. When we approached, the woman came out from the hair salon and spoke to the two men in machine-gun speed. I gathered that something happened to the van, but I didn't see any broken window or stolen tires.

Indeed, someone did break into the van and stole the radio and a few other items. That's the power of addiction. When one is desperate to find money for the next fix, one loses all senses. These two gentlemen (and their group of volunteers) are about the only people on God's green earth that give a damn about these forsaken people. And yet the helpers became prey. To my new friends' credit, they were upset more because of the fact that those responsible broke their trust more than the fact that the van was broken into. I offered my meek consolation by pointing out that at least these people had the decency to break open the door skillfully without breaking the window. They easily could have caused more damage to the van than they did. However, the damage to their trust would be too hard to measure. This little incident also brought us back to the very reality in which we found ourselves.

Teeth Tell Tales

I noticed in the Red Zone that at least three adults would be needed to make a complete set of teeth. This is quite a big contrast from what I observed in Costa Rica in the previous months. This country takes care of its teeth and there are more dentists than postmen - in fact, I don't remember seeing any on the street. My tico friends told me that dental surgery is very expensive so they all learn to take good care of their teeth through daily maintenance and regular visits to their oral hygienists. Among the ticos, other than their way above average eyelashes, I would say that teeth would be their second best feature. I was about to chalk what I observed in the Red Zone up to the drug effect.

When I talked to one of my students, I learned that most of the people in the slums were immigrants from Nicaragua. That explained the teeth discrepancy to an extent! Too bad my Spanish is not good enough to discern the accent. And I found out that the children who live there are likely there because their parents couldn't afford any better, regardless of whether or not they are part of the drug scene. This knowledge brought me renewed shock. If this is an improved condition, what was life like in Nicaragua for them? My student told me that here at least they have a way to feed themselves, but back there they would be hungry.

An Uphill Battle

This is an uphill battle no matter how you look at it, but to give up would only worsen the situation, if it could get any worse, really. This group of people in the Volkswagen van rents the church space and comes here four days a week. They concentrate their efforts on drug prevention instead of rehabilitation. They train the youngsters to make artisan products and other practical skills such as sewing. They give the younger kids something to look forward to once a week, providing activities, a snack, a bible story, and some adult attention. Incidentally, this is the brand of Christianity that I wouldn't mind associating myself with at all, if they would let me. For this group of people, I sense that they get the spirit of the biblical teachings. They eat with the tax collectors and hang out with the lepers, unlike most loud mouths I hear on TV who have perfected the art of using the bible as a weapon. Oh, I just realized how high this soap box is and I will soon need some help to get me down. But I am not nearly done yet.

They run a program to teach the women in the neighborhood to become beauticians. The women learn the skills - cutting hair, dyeing hair, performing manicures and pedicures, etc. - in the year long course at the church. Right now there are about 15 students in the program and they meet on Saturday mornings for a few hours. When they graduate, they go to work in the sponsored salon in Heredia to perfect their skills and gain experience. They get to keep 40% of what they bring in. The rest goes to maintain the shop - rent, utilities, tools, dyeing material, etc. The program is very popular with the local women. I am going to have my hair cut by them later this month. I had my hair cut really short in Dallas two weeks ago and don't have anything for them to work with right now. It will cost 1,500 colones, about $3.5.

There was a typing class going on when I returned to the church from the Red Zone. Well, the girls were learning typing from a computer program (Windows 95!!) and their current techniques left a lot to be desired. At this rate, either they will give up out of frustration or they will never achieve any meaningful speed. Neither outcome is pretty. In fact, I was not sure if they had ever seen anyone touch-typing at any substantial speed. So, I offered them a demo and showed them what it is like to type from 40 to 70, 80 words a minute. That did the trick. It captured their curiosity and established my credentials. I proceeded to give them advice concerning how to cultivate good typing habits. They improved more than 100% within a lesson. Now I am officially their new typing instructor.

Kids Do Say The Darnedest Things

These kids, like the ones last Saturday, were very interested in this new Chinese face. When they learned that I was from Hong Kong, they all asked if I knew Jacky Chan and some other Asian movie stars that they know of. They were quite disappointed when I said no. I should have lied just to make their day. But Jacky Chan wasn't even what interested them the most. My marital status was.

Literally any kid that I spent some time talking with asked me if I was married. No. Then they wanted to know if I had a girlfriend in

America. No. How about Hong Kong? No. How about Costa Rica? No, again. I couldn't help myself and asked one such inquisitor how old he was. He was particularly persistent. He said 10. I asked him why, at such a young age, he was obsessed with my being single. He shrugged and didn't have an answer. By then, I decided that I must be the only 40 year-old single, and Chinese, man that they have ever met in their lives. But what's special about their background that triggered such an uncommon question (from children)?

My New Heroes

During the day, Ronald and I commented that what a shame it was that they didn't find me or I didn't find them earlier. I agreed. On the way home, I thought that it wasn't necessarily a bad thing. The truth is that if I worked in this environment/condition earlier in the year when my immune system was rather compromised, I am not sure if I could have survived the harshness. It could have done me in.

I told them that I would do whatever I could to help out during my last month in Costa Rica. In light of my other current commitments, we agreed that I would be working with them on Tuesdays and Fridays, teaching the typing program, chatting with the teens, playing with the kids, and then cleaning up after them. I really don't have much more to offer than this at the moment. I really ought to learn some skills that are useful for children. These people have done this for years and they are definitely my new heroes. I feel really honored to ride in the same van with them, even though it lacks the peace logo.

40. Update On Work & Puerto Viejo Revisited

June 17, 2005 – San Jose, Costa Rica

I have been occupied, but I must get busy with these journal entries or I will fall so behind that it will be impossible to stay current anymore. I have gotten more involved with the new church that I found and spent 3 days with them this week. I now have a total of 11 typing students - all women; most of them dress a bit too distractingly for some men.

I am still playing with the kids and picking up after them. Even though I am never slow to make them behave, I think they have started to like their new Chinese friend, especially after I gave in and told one group that Jacky Chan is my neighbor. They kept asking! Well, he certainly lives closer to me than to them! Impressed, they proceeded to ask if I knew Bruce Lee. "Net yet" was my response. "Not too soon" is my hope.

Multi-Tasking - An Unusual Combination

One morning, they asked me if I could fix one of their computers - the mouse didn't work. The computer runs Windows 95; I should be glad that it's not Windows 3.1, I suppose. Do you know how tricky it is to fix a mouse problem when the mouse is not working? You can only navigate using key strokes! While I was looking at the problem, and trying to eliminate the possible causes, a baby was dropped on my lap. I distinctly remember that he had four baby teeth. They stood out in my mind. He's a good baby and it took him no time to feel comfortable with me. I found myself holding the baby with my right hand, while trying to diagnose the computer problem with my left hand. The baby just stayed with me quietly and finally I couldn't help taking pictures of us. I thought to myself that I could be a father - even just a single father.

I was done with the computer when the typing students arrived. But the woman who dropped the baby in my lap was nowhere in sight. So, I proceeded to teach the class with the baby in my arms, rocking him gently and singing a Chinese lullaby to keep him calm. It didn't look very professional. It actually looked rather comical, but nobody complained. An hour passed, and I started to wonder if this was one of those "finders, keepers" situations. The baby started to cry and I finally located the woman downstairs in the kitchen, cooking. I wasn't sure if the baby needed some "input" or if he just had some "output." I confirmed that he was hungry.

In the afternoon, I went to meet with the older kids (8-14). These three kids (Carlos, Marcos, & Jorge) arrived early and I sat down at their little table and chatted with them. They are all in the 4th grade and all of them like mathematics. I gave them a little quiz and found that their curriculum was a bit behind that of Hong Kong. We were converting between fractions and decimals in the 4th grade, often in our heads, when I was in Hong Kong. Given their interest in mathematics, I taught them one of my tricks - calculating the day of the week using fingers. They were quick learners and they were able to accurately find out the day of the week their respective birthdays fell on this year. And Christmas too.

I saw them 4 days later at a small evangelical event, and they remembered what I had taught them. They seem like really good kids. Marcos, the 5th of 6 kids in his family, told me that he gets up at 4 every morning to help his mother getting the baby sister ready by giving her a bath and making her smell nice while his mother gets breakfast ready and goes to work. He said he gets to sleep in on Saturdays, until about 6 o'clock!

Update On The Ultimate Brave Souls In Puerto Viejo

When my friend Maurice came to visit from Dallas, he specifically wanted to go to Puerto Viejo in the Caribbean. He really liked the pictures I posted on the website from my previous visit. I enjoyed the place, so it suited me really well. Besides, I have promised Ann & Reid (the original people who brought me to this corner in Costa Rica) that I would return to Puerto Viejo to check on the ultimate brave souls before leaving this country for good.

You may remember that I have written about this young couple (Dan & Jael) from Minnesota who came down to open a restaurant, called Bread & Chocolate. I had the pleasure of chatting with them again last week. Here's what I learned.

Back in January, the flood came the day after we left Puerto Viejo; it was the day of the grand opening of the restaurant. It was also the weekend for the $5,000 surfing contest. As a result of the flood, the roads where blocked and there was no bus coming or going. The tourists were stuck in this little town. A lot of the other restaurants were closed because they were flooded. Dan & Jael's restaurant was built on an elevated platform, so it was spared by the water. The place, however, was flooded with stuck tourists for 3 days. Imagine your grand opening, coupled by this totally unexpected crowd; it wasn't easy. Besides, Jael was already 6 months pregnant by then. She said she was literally holding her stomach with one hand while serving the customers with the other. Incidentally, the food is excellent in this place.

Three days later, the roads were re-opened and people started to leave. The TV news kept reporting how flooded the province was and all the local tourists (it was peak season for them, being summer vacation) went to the Pacific side as a result. The place was a ghost town for quite a well.

Sam, their first baby, was born at home (above the restaurant) on April 11, with the help of two local mid-wives. These people are much braver than I had originally thought. Jael said she didn't like the philosophy of the local hospitals as they discourage natural birth at any sign of delay. Dan's mother was there when the baby was born. Sam is, of course, a tico because he was born in Costa Rica. Dan and Jael now have a first-degree tico relative who can sponsor them for residence/immigration purposes. The adventurous spirit of some people really touches me.

41. Tico Sex & Gender

June 20, 2005 San Jose, Costa Rica

Piropos [pee-RAW-paws]

Piropos is a Latin social phenomenon. It is a noun and it means the very act of men flirting with women who are strangers on the street. From what I understand, these men do not necessarily intend to get to know the women, so it's not the same as pick-up lines in the bars. Often, it is done by drivers (regardless of whether they are driving a car, a taxi, a bus, or even an ambulance) when they see some good-looking women on the street. My impression is that the terms "good-looking" and "scantily dressed" are mostly interchangeable as far as piropos are concerned. These men do their piropos by tapping their horns twice to get the attention of the women. Most women have learned not to turn their heads when this happens.

I was interested in the women's point of view, so I went to ask a few women (about 8) how they like piropos. Some women don't like it at all no matter how it is done. No one likes it when it's done by drivers tapping their horns. Likewise, no one likes the obscene type of piropos. However, rather to my surprise, some actually welcome them, especially if the men talk to them nicely. I asked for a few samples of what the men commonly say for my own reference and here are some statements:

No sabía que del cielo cayó una estrella. (*I didn't know that a star fell from the sky.*)

Del cielo cayó un pañuelo, bordado de mil colores, en el centro decía bonita _____ de mis amores. (*A handkerchief dropped from the sky, embroidered in thousands of colors, and in the center it said pretty "fill in the woman's name here" of my loves*)

I suppose, when it is done right, piropos make a man feel more like a man and woman more a woman. Otherwise, why bother? But not all men are man enough in the eyes of other men.

"Él Es Nada Masculino." (There's nothing masculine about him.)

These, my friends, are the exact words used to describe me by a colleague of one of my tica family members. One day back in April, I came home to find this group of visitors. They were Alvaro's colleagues. One man and his wife. Another man and his girlfriend. They all work together in Guapiles, a city 35 miles northeast of San Jose.

Alvaro leaves home Monday mornings and returns Thursday nights, not unlike my flying consulting friends. By North American standards, it would be inconceivable not to go home every night if you work 35 miles away from home. However, here in Costa Rica, this journey easily takes more than two hours by bus, or by car. The roads can be treacherous and the seemingly "scheduled" afternoon downpour in the rainy season deters the casual drivers. While it is possible to spend 4-5 hours on the daily commute, it's a sheer waste of time and energy. So, he stays there during the week and works from home on Fridays.

Back to my story, I met with the four visitors, and one man was particularly interested in my background as a Chinese man. He asked me a lot about Jacky Chan, Bruce Lee, and such. The standard questions. Do we have better international models/heroes other than these two? Children and adults alike ask about them. How about the two Chinese Nobel prize winners in physics? We Chinese need to do better to promote other heroes other than these two. Not that there's anything wrong with them, but they are not nearly at the top on my list of favorite (Chinese) people.

Back to my story, again. The other man didn't say much to me. I didn't think much of it. The following week, he commented to Alvaro in the office that "él es nada masculino" when my name came up in their conversation. I don't want to know why they talked about me to start with. Alvaro was rather offended by the comment. And he related the story to me. He said his colleague didn't necessarily make any innuendo of any kind, but it was inappropriate, nonetheless, as he didn't know me or Alvaro that well. Alvaro proceeded to tell me something more interesting for me.

In Central America, the men in these countries (like Nicaragua, Honduras, Guatemala, El Salvador, etc.) think that there are no "men" in Costa Rica, and there are only women. What they mean is that the men in Costa Rica do not meet their "masculine" image. Incidentally, the colleague who made the comment happened to be an immigrant from Nicaragua. Like I said in a previous entry, the literacy rate is much higher here than in the other Central American countries, and men have learned to treat women with more respect – comparatively speaking, piropos aside.

In the other countries, women are often treated poorly, both physically and mentally. Besides, generally, well-educated people tend to behave differently. They fight in their lives, but more in the realm of office power struggles, than in the sense of picking street fights. They get drunk, but they don't all spend the night lying on the street as they can afford to take a cab home. And they are mostly able to finish a sentence without using the Spanish equivalent of the "F-word" in mixed company. And so on and so forth. As a result, the tico men are viewed as not manly in this region. Considering the source, and the cultural background, I get a good laugh out of the statement made about me. And I learned something from it. Not bad.

If they are so manly, then I need someone to explain my next (maybe not so) strange observation to me.

Transvestite Phenomenon

Late one night I went home from downtown in a taxi, sitting in the front passenger bucket seat. When we reached the corner near the Don Carlos Hotel, the driver almost hit two pedestrians - slim, leggy, in high heels and short skirts. He seemed to do it to intimidate them; I was annoyed. The women were obviously "working."

After we passed them, the driver asked me if I thought they were pretty. I mumbled the unintelligible "yeeeh uh," properly translated as "you macho idiot, did I give you any sign that I am interested in having a conversation with you?" Not being the sharpest knife in the drawer, he didn't get the clue. And I was smart enough not to verbally upset him - anything can happen to a taxi passenger in the middle of the night. He went on to tell me that these were men, not women. My hushed "oh?" encouraged him. Since he wouldn't shut up anyway, I figured I might as well learn something from him. After all, he drives a cab and has probably seen more in his life than I have.

I asked if their clientele were male or female. I think it's a legitimate question; anatomically, this particular group of sex workers can fill either role. He said the clients are, of course, male. There was no turning back in this conversation at that point. I needed to know if the clients know what they are getting themselves into (if you think I have intended any pun here, your mind is dirtier than mine). Yes, they know.

Then I got the whole story for the duration of my ride home. The clients are closeted gay men, often married. They think it's wrong to have same-sex sex. (I guess the national Catholic teaching has a certain grip on this one and the result is internalized homophobia.) But their hormones tell them otherwise. So, the solution is that they go out at night and find these transvestites to fulfill their sexual needs. If the other party is dressed like a woman, has long hair like a woman, wears panty hose and high heels, then the sex somehow feels less dirty for them and thus more acceptable psychologically. Somehow I have an inkling that these same men might have the loudest voice in any anti-gay campaign. Just a guess. These are not the words of the driver; (he only speaks Spanish. This is the cleaned up version of what he told me, rather like the "artist's rendition."

Shortly after that, I read about the city cleaning up the transvestite sex workers "problem" in San Jose, and some of the said workers are moving to Cartago, a city further east from here, to free themselves of the hostile police force. The scale is much larger than I had ever expected. That's why I call it a phenomenon. Please be clear that I am not making a judgment call of any kind here; rather, I am merely making a social observation.

Now, if you have stayed with me and read this far, you have earned the right to call me "sick," if you haven't done so already. However, I fancy myself as "intellectually curious."

42. Tico Tele-Communications

June 23, 2005 San Jose, Costa Rica

Phone Company

About 10 years ago, I established a quick and easy method to estimate if a country is relatively developed and rich. This theory isn't so bullet proof these days because of the changes in the telecommunication industry, but it still works to an extent.

Instead of digging up GNP data (I never subscribed to how they reach those numbers anyway when I was studying economics), I go to the phone book and check the cost per minute long distance rate to that country. For instance, from the US, until recently, it had long been substantially cheaper to call Hong Kong and Japan than to call China. It's still generally expensive to call most African countries. Calling western Europe costs less than 10 cents a minute. A call to Easter Island or Christmas Island can run $5-10 a minute. With the opening up of the market to competitions, the cost of phone calls has been dropping in most countries, except those with a monopolistic approach to the telecommunication services.

Hong Kong is a perfect case in point. I used to pay $1.5 a minute to call the US in the 80s when there was only one service provider. The same phone call can now be had for as low as 4 cents, while anything above 10 cents is considered to be on the high side these days. Now if someone challenges you to tell them something that doesn't get more expensive over the years, tell them "telephone calls." But not everybody enjoys the same substantial drop in rates. Ask a tico.

ICE - Instituto De Comunicaciones Y Electricidad

Here in Costa Rica, the telephone company is a monopoly. The ICE [EE-say] is a public entity. It's the sole provider for both land-based and mobile phone services, as well as electricity. (Incidentally, this is not unlike the way that computer science studies belonged to the department of mathematics in the universities in the old days. You seldom see them organized that way anymore, just like you seldom see the power company offer phone services in countries where these two services are privatized. But I digressed.) The country is small enough that all phone calls are local calls, so there is no domestic long distance service. It simplifies matters, though the local calls do carry a nominal charge per minute. There is no area code either. Everyone has a 7-digit dialing service. The 4 million people share less than 1 million possible phone numbers. For the sake of comparison, there are roughly 8 million people in Hong Kong, and everybody has 8-digit dialing. So, there are 10 times the phone numbers available for double the population.

Its fully owned subsidiary - RACSA - is the provider for internet services. It seemingly has a monopoly in this market as well. Lately I found out that my language school's internet comes from a cable company - AMNET. You can get cable internet, but the provider is still RACSA (they use AMNET's infrastructure). So, if you want to connect to the internet, you are at the mercy of ICE.

Cellular Phones (Or Mobile Phones, Or Handies Or Celular In Spanish)

What gets my attention is the cellular services. Currently, there are NO phone numbers available. You read it right. You can't get a phone number anymore. If you want to get a cell number, you will have to get on a waiting list. My friend Alonso was on the list back in early 2000 for two years. Currently, the waiting period is about 7 months. So, yes, you can go to the phone company and sign up, and they will tell you when your number will be available. Somehow I remember that while you are on the waiting list, even though you don't have a number, you can still have a cell phone that makes outgoing calls. You just can't receive calls using the phone because the phone simply doesn't have a number associated with it. I don't think it's half bad.

I once went to a talk organized by the language school and the guest was from ICE. He said that there were numbers available still, but the capacity of the system could not keep up with the demand. Therefore, they could only release numbers as the capacity was increased. Back in January, I found out that there were TDMA numbers available. If I had wanted GSM, I would have had to join the waiting list. Alvaro and I went to buy a phone. With the receipt of purchase (to prove that I didn't steal the phone from someone on the street), I got a phone number under his name. The package (clearly there are two choices: 1. Do you want it? 2. Or not?) comes with 60 minutes of free calls for a month. And the monthly charge is about 4,000 colones, or $9. I am not sure about the charge for extra minutes, but my impression is that it's not that unreasonable, though not exactly cheap. My phone bill has yet to exceed $11 over the previous 5 months. SMS (short message services?) are very cheap, so I use the phone that way with my tico friends much more than I use it to talk. Unfortunately, ICE is threatening to raise the charge for SMS soon, due to the popular demand of the service. You just can't win when you are dealing with a monopoly.

Internet

Internet service is becoming more popular, but still, it is not uncommon for a young person to be without service at home. I have recently made a new friend, a UCR (Univ. of CR) senior, a music major specializing in piano performance, who doesn't have internet access at home. In his case, my impression is that it's more of a personal choice. He practices the craft of classical music. And I feel that computers are just not high on his list of interests. However, for most college students, not having internet access at home seems to be the norm rather than the exception. And the cost of a good computer requires some serious financial sacrifice for the students. Personally, I can't run my modern life without the internet, let alone the computer. Everything that I do is somehow tied to the computer and/or internet one way or the other. Cable/DSL runs at about $45-50 a month - or 10% or more of an average worker's monthly income. High speed internet is still a luxury item in this country while dial-up service is slowly becoming a commodity. It's not there yet.

One thing worth mentioning (up till now, I feel like I am just babbling with no substance) is that your dial-up internet service is tied to your home phone number. In other words, your log on ID and password to RACSA only works when you are dialing from home. If you want to be able to dial in from multiple locations, there's a premium to the basic charge. The last time I heard, the basic charge is slightly less than $20 a month. Do keep in mind, $20 is not a lot for an American household, but it's the budget for food for more than 10 days for a family of 5 that I know of here. It's all relative.

I didn't quite understand why ICE bothered to lock down an ID/password with the home phone at the beginning. Now that I have learned more about the cost of living and income level and such, I can see that any Jose may be inclined to share the same log-on among several cousins and uncles. And can you blame them? Keep in mind, though, there is a per-minute usage charge because you are using your phone to connect to the internet. I have run up quite a bill for my family. Even though I pay the difference between the current bill and their average bill before my arrival, my tica family is still shocked at how much I spend on communications. The average bill is now 5 times bigger than what it was in October! What can I say? I need to upload those hundreds of photos and a slow internet takes time! And I like to stay in touch with the world via the internet and e-mail. While I am utterly grateful for the dial-up internet access, I DO miss DSL.

43. Tico Life II

June 24, 2005 – San Jose, Costa Rica

Supplement To Piropos – A Male Perspective

I shared my entry about piropos with my pianist friend Erick, and he decided I needed the male perspective on this matter as well, which I think is totally fair. And he made a few very good points. This is what I learned form Erick. The person who does the piropo has a lot to do with how it will be received. Piropos from older gentlemen and good-looking men stand a better chance. In other words, if a woman doesn't feel that her safety is being threatened when a piropo is directed toward her, she receives the piropo with a much more positive attitude.

He further explained that the large majority of the men don't create piropos of their own. Generally, piropos come from songs. When the men see that a line is used in a song, they perceive that it is safe to use it when they make piropos. This wasn't a bad rule when songs were written with a more reserved attitude and lyrics were more like poems. Nowadays, some pop songs can be so grotesque that they are not suitable to be played in mixed company. But some men still stick to the old rules. As a result, piropos are getting a bad reputation these days.

Shopping

I have meant to write about shopping a long time ago. Better late than never. Well, if you have a car in San Jose, half of your shopping can be done while you are driving around town. There are people, mostly Nicaraguan immigrants, selling things at the intersections of the major thoroughfares. There are plenty of them. They sell anything from newspapers, snacks, pens and pencils, fresh fruit and vegetables, sunglasses or umbrellas (never at the same time), cell phone battery chargers using the cars AC/DC outlet (I thought that was clever - right product and right place to sell it), and many other things in between, including lottery tickets.

But what I want to talk about here is how the stores work, when it comes to paying. Unless you are buying from a really small shop of any kind (i.e. you are likely dealing with the owner directly, fast food chains excepted, among a few others), you almost never pay who serves you. There's always a full-time cashier sitting in the corner, in a semi-protected glass box. I think the separation of duties give the owners a better sense of control and minimizes the risk of being robbed by the employees themselves. I imagine that cashiers must have some references before they can get the job.

A few years ago, when I was trying to buy a CD at a department store, I experienced the highest security ever. Upon entering the store, I had to check my knapsack (backpack) at a counter. The CDs were all locked up. Some were locked up in a display device that the shopkeepers had to use an electric screwdriver to open and shut. Others were locked up in drawers. My impression was that if you didn't know what you were looking for, you probably would never find it.

After I decided what I wanted, a shopkeeper unlocked a drawer and found my CD. Another shopkeeper wrote an invoice, and I was to pay the cashier for the merchandise at the front of the store. While I was paying, a third shopkeeper was wrapping up my CD. When I returned with my receipt, I got my purchase. One transaction, four people. My friend told me that it was because they did not have the theft prevention devices set up in the CD section yet. Still, it's only a CD, for crying out loud. What would happen if they were to sell diamonds in that store? To be fair, the other departments function more like a regular department store anywhere else in the world. I think CDs suffer a higher pilferage rate because of the potential customers that the commodity attracts – hence the extra precaution. Fortunately, all the people were very friendly, and it was not a bad way to practice Spanish. I actually quite enjoyed the experience.

I went to the post office this afternoon to buy some stamps. (Speaking of stamps, here, stamps are only printed when they are sold - you will notice that there is a date on the stamp if you should be so lucky to have received a postcard from Costa Rica.) And I noticed that there were quite a few security guards in the lobby and some of them had pistols. I wasn't sure if there's that much money in a post office, albeit the main one. In shops where the items are highly priced, like one of the sports equipment stores in San Pedro, they actually hire security guards with rifles. The sight is actually quite intimidating.

Naming Your Kids

Spanish speaking countries are by default all Catholic countries; I can't think of any Spanish speaking country that is not officially Catholic. Maybe Equatorial Guinea in west Africa? Well, it is not unusual at all to meet Jesús [hay-SOOS]. Of course, I don't mean Jesus from the Bible. Many people name their children Jesús. This is an interesting cultural difference for me. They like and respect their Jesus so much that they want their sons to be just like one of the trinity. If they are a little less ambitious, they go for José and María, before going down the list of apostles. Likewise, the Islamic culture likes to name their boys Mohammed - making Mohammed the most popular name in the world. When I was working at the International Admissions Office in college, I had a hard time filing the Pakistani applications. You wouldn't believe how many Mohammed Syeds we had in the cabinet at any given time. I don't know what their secret of telling one another apart on paper is. I certainly was pulling my hair out matching transcripts with applications.

At the other end of the spectrum, we Chinese avoid naming our children after people that we respect, for fear that our children would bring shame to the name. Meanwhile, I have never met an Anglo American Jesus. Though Americans' idea seems to be much closer to the idea held by many in the Hispanic culture. They would name their kids after anyone in the Bible except the big guy, and also maybe except Judas. They also name their kids after themselves – hence the Mr. So & So Jr. III, IV..... Personally, I have a hard time accepting the fact that I should change my name (to Andy Pang Sr.) because I have a son.

The funny thing is that all the different cultures are trying to do exactly the same thing - behave in a way that is respectful toward the people they admire and respect. However, different cultures do it differently, even in directly opposing manners, as demonstrated in this case. Next time, before I make a cultural judgment call, I will make sure that the people aren't just doing the same thing, in spite of what meets the eyes.

44. Pianoforte – My First Love

June 26, 2005 – San Jose, Costa Rica

Since the beginning of the sabbatical, I have been thinking about what extra-curricular passion to pursue when this sabbatical year is over. I have spent many years learning Spanish on and off and it's time for something else. The answer came very early in the year, loud and clear: it's piano.

Then I met Erick, a young, recently married pianist at the Grand Hotel, the oldest hotel in San Jose.

My friend Alonso and I went to have dinner one night at the Grand Hotel a few weeks ago. Erick was playing that night and he was very good. I went back to listen to him with another friend. That time, I wrote down four songs as my requests; he played two of them and didn't have the music for Somewhere In Time & Eighteenth Variation. He's never heard of the songs (those are not very popular songs and he was a toddler when Somewhere In Time came out). I asked him if he wanted to hear Somewhere In Time; he asked me if I played. "Not very well" was my response. He let me play the song anyway, right there in the lobby of a restaurant half full of patrons.

Over the next few weeks, he had shown me how he sight-read and how he changed the accompaniment in the second part of a song, as well as how he filled in the spaces and improvised popular songs. I happened to pick two songs out of the book that he had never even heard of, and he played them like he had grown up with them. That was very impressive. Erick is in his final semester at UCR, pursuing a bachelor's degree in music, with emphasis in piano performance. And he speaks English reasonably well, which made our conversation about music and piano possible.

I have a few friends in the US and Hong Kong who have degrees in piano, including one with a Ph.D. in Piano Performance, and all of these people have refused to play anything for me. In fact, I have never heard them play. The Ph.D. guy actually said that he couldn't play the piano just because I asked. That would have been an insult to his art. And that would be equivalent to asking Andre Agassi to play tennis with me, if Andre were a friend of mine. Whatever that meant! I was dumb-founded and didn't know what to say, and hence didn't say anything. Incidentally, I no longer am in contact with this person.

My history with accomplished pianists was disheartening, to say the least. Because of these experiences, I was extremely grateful to Erick for his kindness. Granted, he works for the hotel and he played what I requested as a professional courtesy. But, he did much more beyond his call of duty. I was glad to find a professional pianist who doesn't think he is too good to entertain the curiosity of a beginner. He even gave me copies of music that he thought would be a good challenge and source of motivation for me. To top it off, he allowed me to record a song, a beautiful Costa Rican song called Sonata Para Un Atardecer (Sonata For An Evening), on video while he demonstrated it. My goal is to learn to play that song within five years.

Ever since I saw a piano the first time in elementary school, I have been in love with it. It truly was my first love. However, there was no way that my parents could afford piano lessons for me, let alone buying a piano. There's no room for it anyway. I was given a piano when I was twenty; this family had no use for the piano and it was given to them years earlier. I started to teach myself to read music and played for two years. Then I hired a teacher when I could afford it, yet I fired the teacher at the end of the first month. He hit my fingers with a pencil and he wasn't even a good pianist himself. I went to another woman, and she lasted two months.

In Hong Kong, they mainly teach to prepare the students for the Royal School of Music examinations. They generally charge by the grade that you are preparing for. I was an adult student and I could care less about what the Royal School of Music thought of my ability, but that's the only thing they knew how to teach. In short, the teachers that I had were uninspiring and mediocre.

I then became a tour guide, and the traveling made regular piano practice very difficult, if not impossible. When I finished college and moved back to Texas, I bought a piano before I bought a bed. I slept on the floor for two years, but I had a piano at the beginning of the second year, but again, no money for lessons as I was paying off my academic debts. Later on, when money was available, I opted for a master's degree, followed by the acquisition of Spanish. In other words, I have betrayed my first love for 34 years. It's time I go back to my first love when I come back to live in Texas at the end of this sabbatical. I will find a way to make it work in spite of the travel demands of my job. It will be good for my soul.

Let me take this opportunity to say something about traveling from my own experience. What makes a trip memorable for a long time is always the human contact that I make. Beautiful sights abound around the world, but what truly makes a spot stand out in my mind in the end is the people that I have come in contact with in these far away places. Fortunately, I learned this lesson very early in my travel, in my early 20s. I watched Rick Steves about two months ago on TV and he made the very same comment. And we didn't even talk before he taped the show!

45. My Fear Of Working With Children

June 27, 2005 – San Jose, Costa Rica

I haven't written this story until now because I don't want people to worry about me more than they already do and I don't want to complicate my relationship with my host family. All along, it was my intention to work with children. Last September, before I left the US, I happened upon this documentary on A&E about an older gentleman from southern California who had been helping an orphanage in Baja California for more than five years on and off before he was falsely imprisoned for child sexual abuse. After spending twelve years in jail, he was finally proved not guilty and released. The children who pointed the fingers were coerced by the local man in charge of the orphanage to make the false accusation in court; in fact, they didn't have to appear in court. They just made a statement. The local man in charge was stealing money from the funds and his crime was about to be discovered. With this story fresh in my mind, I came to Costa Rica.

When I first arrived, my host family told me that it would be impossible for me to be accepted by any organization to work with children because of my being a single male. My later attempt to contact a local Catholic order - the Salesians, the same order that ran my high school in Hong Kong - proved that my family was not entirely wrong. In fact, the church didn't return my e-mails or phone calls. In my mind, I thought it was extremely ironic that they were the ones paying millions of dollars to settle outside the court for their very act of abusing children for years on end, and now they ignored my inquiries. At about the same time, my interviews with the state orphanages went well, I thought, but the promised phone calls never came.

On the first weekend I was here, I was invited to a birthday party at the house of a college friend of my host family. They had known each other for more than fifteen years. It was a cold evening, in early December, and we had a barbecue outside. I met the friend that morning when we went shopping in his construction materials store. There were signs of religious sayings everywhere in the store. The man was obviously very Catholic. Later that night I met his wife and two boys, age 11 & 15, at their house. In spite of the very cold weather, the party stayed outside, about 10 steps from the entrance to the living room. They had an organ in the living room, and I asked the father who the organist was in the family. It was the younger son, and he said we could play. I told him I would like to hear what his son was learning for Christmas after we ate. Our hands were sticky from the barbecue. The mother was not part of this conversation.

There were about 10 adults in this party. When we finished eating, everyone was so cold that you could hear teeth chattering. The younger son and I went inside the living room (the door was never closed), and he played the Christmas carols that he was learning. The older son was playing video games in his own room, located about 4-5 steps from the living room. Meanwhile, the party went on, about 10 steps away from where we were. They could hear us and the organ loud and clear. The mother came in and got a sweater and returned to watch us a few times. After we finished playing, the young son wanted me to go play video games with him in his bedroom. I told him no. That wouldn't be appropriate. And I returned to the party and didn't think much of anything. We left the party and went home before midnight, and before we were frozen.

At breakfast the next morning, my host family said, "Let me tell you something about the culture here." I distinctly remember it sounded as bad as "we have to talk," or the unfolding of a "Dear John" letter. When the young boy and I disappeared into the living room the night before (*I should remind you, for the third time, we were merely 10 steps away from the 9 adults outside, and the door was open*), the mother immediately turned to my friend and asked, "Es confiable?" or "Is he trustworthy?" My friend, of course, said "yes" but was nevertheless very embarrassed because of me. Come to think of it, he must have been pretty mad at me that night because he didn't relate this to me until the next morning. The ride home took almost an hour. We had plenty of time.

My friend said I really needed to think before I act. He reminded me that because of the child abuse cases in recent years in Costa Rica, including those involving the Catholic priests, (and especially because of those involving the priests, I would think) the people are terrified to leave their children alone with strangers. I really wanted to defend myself by telling them the whole event and that I wasn't a complete stranger; I came to the party with a friend of the parents whom they had known for 15 years. And the kid and I were only 10 steps away from the adults and the door was open and they could hear us. The father approved beforehand. And the older brother was in the next room. But what good would it do? I obviously made a mistake, albeit unbeknown to me, even though I still think the woman over-reacted. I learned my lesson and gained some new perspective on my situation.

I feel sorry for the mother. The night before, they were asking me about colleges in America or England as they wanted to send their son to college in an English speaking country. They certainly could afford it. The son had his eye on University of Miami at Corals Gable, Florida. They asked me how the college atmosphere was, especially about the drug and sex scene (like I knew anything about either!) and how the crime was, in general, in America. And they felt that the son would be in better hands if he should go to school in England or Canada instead. I told them not to trust everything they saw on TV. After this incident, I think she will worry herself sick if her older son does end up in college outside of Costa Rica.

After breakfast, we went to visit another friend who lived nearby and there was a five year-old boy - the grandson of the friend. I have met this friend once or twice in my prior visits, and my trustworthiness was more established! I tried to make minimal contact with the kid - waving in the distance, not initiating conversations, and so on. But he took a liking to me. A lot of kids do. I think it's because they feel that I am one of them. I laugh and giggle and get mad and am silly just as easily as they. He wanted me to go into his room and play with his new toys, a set of construction trucks. My friends witnessed the request. I shrugged and told the kid to bring the toys out to the living room instead.

I had practically given up hope of working with (disadvantaged) children after all these situations, until later on when I met the group in Guarari, Heredia. But you already know that.

46. Tico Life III

June 29, 2005 – San Jose, Costa Rica

Tico Season / Weather

Costa Rica is physically located in the northern hemisphere. However, according to the ticos, it's now winter in Costa Rica. And summer will start in late November, or early December. I always thought that if you were in the northern hemisphere, then your summer would start on June 22 - the Summer Solstice. Not so for Costa Rica. There's another thing that is anti-intuitive about the classification of seasons. It's cooler, sometimes down right cold, and drier in the summer. And winter is wet and warmer.

I have been wondering why their nomenclature of the seasons contradicts that of USA or Hong Kong, both located north of the equator. This brought to mind the school year calendar. Instead of the September till June (e.g. 2004-2005) calendar that is popular in the US, the Costa Rican school year starts in February and ends in November. Their summer vacation coincides with Christmas in the drier season, and their academic year also goes hand-in-hand with the calendar year. So, I imagine that the drier season is also the season for harvest. Hence, in the good old days, schools had to be closed so that the kids could help with the harvest. And, therefore, the summer vacation. Could that be it? At any rate, this is my theory and I am sticking to it until I have further information to believe otherwise.

Speaking of weather, the rainy season is upon us and when it rains in the tropics, it literally pours, sometimes for hours on end. And rain is a daily event until late November or even early December, mostly in the afternoons and into the late evenings. This downpour makes the already pot-hole infested roads even more treacherous. The auto shops have a lot more repair business during the rainy season.

On a remotely related note, there's a Ferrari dealership in Curridabat. Who buys Ferraris here? More importantly, what is the point of driving a Ferrari at 30-40 MPH most of the time? The buses are slow and sometimes you have to make connections to get to your destination. I have spent many an hour riding them in town. Because of these problems with the buses, everyone wants a car. Meanwhile, there is little infrastructure expansion and improvement. I predict that the traffic in San Jose will resemble that of Bangkok in not too many years. Not a pretty outlook.

Currencies

Even though the official currency is colones, the US$ is accepted in many places. This includes the medium-haul distance buses, like those from San Jose to the Caribbean. When I first came here in 1999, the exchange rate was $1=330 colones. This week, it is 475 colones. The colones has been losing value over the years. There are talks of officially dollarizing the economy, i.e., adopting the dollars as its official currency. I believe, in addition to Panama, Ecuador has done that (or some other Latin America country).

My impression is that highly priced items are listed in US dollars. Therefore, when you buy a nice condo in Escasu, the price comes out in dollars. Cars are also often quoted in dollars. When you borrow money to buy your house and if your loan is in dollars, the APR is about 8%. Conversely, if your loan is in colones, the rate can be as high as 20% or even higher.

Family Size

The guide for the tour to the rain forest said that an average family in Costa Rica has 1.5 kids. At this rate, they are not sustaining the population. And I infer that they are not following the Catholic Church's teaching of staying away from contraceptive measures. I take it as a sign that this country is growing economically. Only in semi-developed & developed countries can we find that the children become financial liabilities instead of financial assets. Look at the US, western Europe, Japan, Hong Kong, Singapore. You see this pattern.

On a related note, the wife of one of my fellow tico volunteers came from a family of 18 children, and there is only one set of twins. The poor mother was pregnant at least 17 times, assuming there were no miscarriages. Or as I would like to say, her stomach has never been empty since she married that man. I suppose her parents can be the poster child(ren) for the Catholic church's policy on contraception.

Where Are You From?

This question will become much easier to answer when I get to Hong Kong. In fact, nobody will ask! It isn't so simple a question in Costa Rica. My friends like to introduce me as their American friend from Texas. If the other party speaks good English, they would wonder where my Texas drawl went. When I am given the opportunity to answer this question directly, I always say: "I was born in Hong Kong, but I have been living in the States since 1989." I like answering questions in complete form. Personally, I think it's much more interesting for the ticos to meet someone from Hong Kong than from Texas. I don't mean to say that the Texans are not interesting, but the ticos have met a lot of gringos, and most of them can't tell a Texan from a Yankee. For them, a gringo is a gringo, but meeting someone from Hong Kong is not so common.

Incidentally, this question was even more complicated when I was on the cruise. Just imagine, I had to cite Hong Kong, Texas, and Costa Rica in one sentence.

One Ply Toilet Paper (And Other Things That I Don't Understand)

There are things that I don't think I will ever understand. Just like I still haven't figured out the purpose of one-ply toilet paper over the last two decades. What good does that do, really? Like I said before, the ticos are a bunch of polite folks, in general. That is, until they dial a wrong number on the phone. Instead of a simple "I am sorry," they just hang up as soon as you tell them that they have made a mistake in dialing. It's very annoying. Once in a blue moon I would hear an "I am sorry." And when that happens, I almost want to keep that person's number (caller ID is popular) and interview him/her later on about what makes them different from the greater society they found themselves in.

Felipe, the toddler who lives next door, celebrated his first birthday last week. At his party, there was a piñata. I have never seen a piñata in action at a party. The kids took turns beating up the cute doll in an attempt to get to the candies and goodies inside. When the doll finally gave way and broke apart, the kids (adults were also invited to participate) fought one another for the goodies. Who invented this idea of piñata? I was horrified at how violent the whole thing was. Now, I can't help wondering if this is the training of turning someone macho? Or does it prepare them psychologically when they learn to drive as adults later on.

Ticos also have a very different face when they drive. People lose their patience and courtesy once they are behind the wheel. I don't know what it is about the automobile that brings out a different side to people. I always thought gambling tables were where you showed your true face. Everyone who lives here knows that the drivers are aggressive. However, when I sit in the front seat of a cab, I often see that people SEEM to be crossing the street without looking. Even the cab drivers agree with me on this. I am leaving soon enough and the issues may eventually show up on Unsolved Mysteries on the cable channel. Until then, I will just have to live with the knowledge that there are some seemingly simple things that I couldn't explain in Costa Rica.

47. There's No Banquet That Doesn't End!

June 30, 2005 – San Jose, Costa Rica

There's No Banquet That Doesn't End!

This is a famous Chinese proverb. We Chinese always say this when we don't want to say good-bye, and occasionally at funerals. This week was filled with farewell parties with different church groups, students, and friends. I obviously have mixed emotions about leaving the country that I have temporarily adopted for the last seven months.

Just when I think I am having the best time, the Costa Rican portion of the sabbatical is coming to a close. It's better this way - departing on a high note instead of painfully counting the number of days before leaving. Looking back, I have these specific thoughts about my extended stay here.

What I Like The Most About Costa Rica & The Least

One of my students treated me to a Chinese dinner as our farewell. I have been busy with expressing my farewells during the last week of my stay. He asked me what I like the most and the least about Costa Rica. I like the people the most. They are generally very friendly and warm. For that very reason, I come back here to visit so often. However, what I like the least about this country also has to do with the people themselves. It's the undercurrent of racism. They may not like to admit it, but I can distinctly feel that Nicaraguans and Colombians are not very popular here. I have also heard derogatory comments about people of darker complexion. The Chinese immigrants are respected because they are hard-working and they run Chinese restaurants, but, due to the language and cultural barriers, they are largely seen as a non-integrated group of the society. The Chinese are very much responsible, as well, to improve this situation.

The State Of My Spanish

Regarding my Spanish language skill, well, it's hard to say. One good thing did happen right around April, and all of a sudden, I was no longer obsessed with Spanish. I can't pinpoint what triggered it but I am glad, as obsession of any kind is not healthy.

I can communicate most thoughts, and what I know how to say, I tend to say it with accurate grammar. I can read the newspaper, magazines, and translated novels and I can understand the stories without consulting the dictionary too often. I understand soap operas to a large extent. I am also one of the few non-native speakers who write better than they speak. I do not have a strong foreign accent, as many people have told me, although my tica family insists that I am distinctly Chinese when I speak Spanish. Vocabulary is still a problem, just like my English. I don't read nearly enough in Spanish to expand my vocabulary. I would say I can handle many situations in Spanish, though I am far from being natively fluent. And my English will forever be far better than my Spanish (at least I hope so since I have spent way too many years learning this impossible language).

It's All About Perspective

I have met a lot of nice people in my last six weeks in Costa Rica. Initially, I felt cheated that I didn't meet these people when I first arrived. Then I saw the light and I realized how wrong this was. The truth is that I am very lucky to have met some really nice people before I left. In fact, the chance was much greater that our paths might not have crossed at all. And the fact that they did cross each other was a blessing to be embraced, rather than something to be lamented. I will miss these people.

Leaving the kids is a different story. I think it can be difficult for them. At the end of June, the gentleman from Honduras and I are leaving at the same time. They have suddenly lost two familiar faces that come and play with them and teach them things. I feel that I have abandoned them like a lot of the male figures, especially their fathers, in their lives. They asked me to stay longer. Then they asked me why I couldn't stay longer. Even the teens and the adults asked the same thing.

I have built a rapport with them. But I can't be here anymore for them, like every other adult that has abandoned them. A deed with good intention can actually bring so much hurt. How ironic! As an adult, I look at it and see that we have had this beautiful time together. But how do you expect a child to understand this? Well, it is not easy for me either. But there's no banquet that doesn't end.

Friendship, Like Love, Is A Gift

You can't force love. I learned this lesson from watching black-and-white movie reruns when I was in grade school. Likewise, you can't force friendship either, but this lesson took me longer to learn. I am just a slow learner in certain areas of life. However, I usually meet a stranger with the mindset that he or she might be one of my future best friends.

With some people you easily become friends. With others, you could live with them for a year, and nothing would happen - like my 3 dormitory roommates in college. We lived together for a year, and in their formative years at that (I was 5 years older), yet I have absolutely no rapport with them. In fact, I don't even know where they live anymore and I don't remember one guy's last name. Coming from someone who keeps pretty decent records, this is a strong testimonial. Then I met my tica family and we became long-term friends. Of all my Spanish teachers that I have had in previous years here, I have become good friends with Gaby. She introduced me to her family and she and I can talk about anything without putting up any front. Then there's Alonso, one of my best tico friends, a young man I met in my first trip through another friend of my tica family. I didn't talk to or see that friend during my entire stay this time. I suppose he's off my Christmas list this year. I really can't afford the time and stamps for one-way communication anymore. The Christmas letter count went over two hundred in the last 2-3 years, and I have been gradually cleaning up my list.

I have met a lot of people through my work with the two different churches. Only time will tell who will remain in my life after I remove myself from Costa Rica.

A Peek Into The Future

My original plan was to leave here and go to Queretaro, Mexico, to spend two months in a women's shelter/orphanage there, but I changed that plan in early May. This year so far, I have given a lot of time to indulge myself. I have also spent a lot of time with people that I have just met. I still don't know what I have done to deserve being so lucky to have these experiences.

However, there is one group of people that I should spend some time with - my own family in Hong Kong. Granted, I visit them almost yearly, but unless I move back to Hong Kong, the next months will likely be the last opportunity for me to spend an extended period of time with my aging parents.

Ironically, I am quite sure that the very majority of my family has not read this website nor seen the pictures therein; it being in English certainly doesn't help the matter. We are not very emotional people. When I arrive there, I certainly do not expect a hug (that will be way too weird in my family), nor a handshake. But I know they will be glad to see me, in spite of the absence of the formalities. Before that, however, I am going to visit my southern parents at their beach house in Florida. On my way to Hong Kong, I will stop in Los Angeles for two days to visit my west coast parents. The following two weeks will see me in many airports and highways.

48. Hong Kong: Homebound, Or Just Visiting?

July 18, 2005 – Hong Kong, China

I arrived in Hong Kong Friday night, 3 days ago. It has been hot, humid, and sunny since my arrival. Mentally, I am really not sure if I am home or if I am just visiting. A clearer answer may surface when this feeling of jetlag is gone. Getting up in the middle of the night for 3 days in a row is not conducive to clear thinking. I left Hong Kong for the US in July 1989, exactly 16 years ago. Both Hong Kong and I have changed a great deal, though not necessarily in the same direction. And the last two whirlwind weeks in the US didn't help matters at all.

On Saturday, I went to my first dim sum meal with my parents, 3 of my sisters, and my younger brother. I don't think that my mother knew that I was in Hong Kong until she saw me at the restaurant. Even after the meal, my mother and I still have not talked. I am sure this is extremely difficult for outsiders to understand. We are not mad at each other or anything, but this is the way it is in my family. So far, I have seen about 60% of my family and it will take a whole month to see everyone, as one of them just left for Beijing for a month-long Mandarin course.

While we were at the restaurant (where my father is a regular), the two waitresses found out that I am related to my father and that I am still single. They immediately threatened to engage in some match-making. I am sure my father has complained to anyone who would listen that both his boys are incapable of finding wives. My 3rd sister Patty later told me that there is a shortage of marriage-worthy single men in Hong Kong. From what she observed and learned from the media, these days the women here as a whole are more hard-working and more career-minded than the men, most of whom just go from being boys to being older boys with more expensive toys.

On one popular radio show, a heartbroken woman called in to seek advice from the hosts. She introduced her boyfriend to her (girl) friends and the boyfriend became her pal's new boyfriend. It happened to her twice. Another girl didn't let any of her single friends know that she was dating until she sent out the wedding invitations.

While I am getting acclimated to the new time zone and the humidity, I will think about how best to continue these journal entries from Hong Kong.

49. Fragrant Harbor I

July 25, 2005 – Hong Kong, China

What's In A Name?

Hong Kong - literally it means Fragrant Harbor. Supposedly, the fragrance came from the incense making industry back in the pre-colonial days. In my grammar school days in the seventies, we were taught that Hong Kong was known as the Pearl of the Orient. Of course, Hong Kong is now officially known as Hong Kong SAR (Special Administration Region). The name was given by Beijing when the sovereignty of Hong Kong was returned to China in 1997.

For the ten years leading up to 1997, I was afraid that the Beijing government might feel the need to change Hong Kong to "Xianggang," its Mandarin phonetics, like Guangzhou for Canton, Beijing for Peking, Xiamen for Amoy, etc. I am looking at it from the marketing point of view. Coca-Cola might add cherry or a hint of lemon to its products, but the "established" name Coca-Cola is never touched. If you want to argue by citing "New Coke" as an example, I rest my case.

Everything Disney

Hong Kong Disney is scheduled to open on September 12. The primary target market is the tourists from mainland China. The subway has a new branch that takes visitors directly to the theme park. The windows of the trains on this line are shaped like Mickey's ears. There will also be ferries from the financial district. One of the local casual clothes chains has already issued its Disney series. The first pop love song featuring Disney is out.

We shall see if it will do the magic the Hong Kong government expected when it seduced Disney into choosing Hong Kong for its second theme park in Asia a few years ago. The locals are quite excited about the forthcoming opening. Over the last few years, the real estate developers have been using Disney as one of the features/attractions for their new developments. Why would one choose a place to live because of its easy access to the theme park? How many times can you go there in a year before it gets old?

Real Estate Market

The real estate market took a dive after the Asian financial crisis at the turn of the millennium and many people ended up owning negative assets – that is, their mortgage is greater than the value of the properties. Later on, the market dropped as much as 40-60% again during and after the SARS (Severe Acute Respiratory Syndrome) crisis in 2003. This city is unbelievably resilient and, from what I can see, the real estate market has already recovered. The front pages of the local papers are often sold as a full-page advertisement to promote a new housing project. Often for a few days at a time. I can't imagine what their advertising budget is for a project.

It's well-known that this is one of the world's most crowded cities, but this doesn't mean there aren't big homes. Where bigger apartments are not available, people have the option to buy two connecting units to make a bigger apartment. Lately, there are some brand new apartments, including free standing houses, which are in excess of 3,000 square feet, at about US$2,000 per square feet. Last week, one of the land developers was selling a duplex on the harbor front, on the 69th and 70th floors, with a total of 10,000 square feet of living space. I have no idea what the listing price is. The concept of money is very different in this city. Some people obviously have a lot and I don't know who they are or what they do.

One thing I don't like about the real estate market here is that when a new project goes on sale, the developer only sells 20 units or so at a time. They pick 20 units from the whole project and test the reaction from the market. If the reaction is good, then they will raise the price immediately for the next batch. In reality, it doesn't affect me as I can't afford any of these. It may be very good business practice, but it's way too calculating for my liking.

The government used to build apartments for sale, from roughly 400-800 square feet each - at about half or less of the market price of a privately developed project of similar quality. Right now, these units run at about US$125-150K each. These apartments do not come with the bells and whistles of the large private projects in which well-equipped club house, swimming pool, private gym and such are the norm. The private developers somehow managed to convince the government to stop providing affordable housing, and the government is now selling the last batch and will discontinue this 20-30 year program. Here in town, buying a house is a life-long effort for the lower-middle class. Some 50% of the people rent apartments from the government, and these units range from 200-500 square feet.

Hong Kong Book Fair, July 21-25

The Hong Kong Trade Development hosts a book fair at the Hong Kong Exhibition Centre (HKEC). The book fair runs from 10 am-10 pm daily. On Saturday, it opened until midnight. This truly is a city that doesn't sleep.

The HKEC opened in 1997 just in time for the transfer of sovereignty ceremony and I have never seen the inside. I took advantage of the occasion to see the building. The book fair is a major success and it is way too crowded for me (630,000 people attended!). When I visited Hong Kong in the past, I often asked myself why I didn't choose to come back to live here. This time, I find myself asking a different question: "why would I even want to live in such a crowded, hot, and humid place?" Going from Costa Rica to Hong Kong requires some more adjustment on my part yet.

Two "Beauty Pageants" In One Week

The day after my arrival, a local TV station hosted the Mr. Asia Contest. I missed the live broadcast. What I found interesting was that there were three representatives from mainland China. Even though it is a big country, I don't think it's fair that they should have more than one representative. At the end of the day, one of these three won the contest. Hong Kong won the first runner-up title, and Israel and China tied for second runner-up. In case you wonder, it works just like Miss Universe (cultural costume, swim suits, questions, and the works). What really drew my attention was that a gentleman from Iraq was in the pageant. How was he chosen in Iraq? How? Really.

Last night, the other local station hosted the Mr. Hong Kong Contest. I missed the live broadcast also. From what I read online, you don't have to be single to qualify. Other than that, it works just like the Miss Hong Kong pageant, almost.

I mentioned in my previous journal entry that the women here complain that there is a shortage of quality men in Hong Kong. Well, maybe they can find them on TV competing for these titles. There is more equality between the sexes in Hong Kong than anywhere else in the world that I know of. I think it's a good thing.

50. Fragrant Harbor II - Medical Practices

July 30, 2005 – Hong Kong, China

Government Proposes Medical Reform

The HK SAR government currently spends one seventh of its budget on medical services. With an aging population, social medicine is quickly becoming a burden for the government. When my father had his colon surgery in a public hospital a few years ago, he spent 17 days in the hospital and it cost him slightly less than US$9 a day, or a total of $150, the cost of the surgery included. The problem is that people are flooding the outpatient emergency room and the government is trying to divert the people who do not have problems that involve some type of emergency to the private practitioners.

For those who don't want to subject themselves to the long waiting period and can afford it, there are very high quality private hospitals, with correspondingly high billing rates, but the regular working class (those without comprehensive medical benefits from their employers) cannot afford it.

The Private Physician Practice

A lot of local general practitioners or family doctors are notorious for the amount of patients they see in a day. The patients traditionally expect a large amount of medicine; otherwise, they consider the doctor less effective. My personal experiences with the local doctors are almost 20 years old, but they contrast sharply with my PCP in Dallas. In Hong Kong, it was "all business." I describe my symptoms and the doctor prescribes medicine. In Dallas, I have a rapport with my doctor; he asks about what I do, my eating, working and exercise habits, yes, and my sex life. It is comprehensive care, and I appreciate that my doctor looks at my health welfare as a total package, not just my symptoms at the time of consultation.

What is worth mentioning is that the Hong Kong people, including the young ones, do not always visit western medical practitioners by default. Depending on the type of illness, sometimes they visit Chinese herbal medicine practitioners. The general perception is that western medicine deals with the symptoms of the illness, whereas herbal medicine deals with the root, or the cause of the illness. The last decade has seen a lot of changes in the status of herbal medicine. The government has created certification programs to legitimize and regulate the practice. Traditionally one learns the art through apprenticeship from a master. These days, there are herbal medicine colleges where one can spend 4-5 years studying and preparing for the certification examination.

Medical Practice Of A Third Kind

When one doesn't recover from an illness within the normal time frame, it is not unreasonable to suspect that the patient, or sometimes his/her family members, has offended a "spirit." The spirit is often the ancestors of the family, though it can also be a stranger. When this is suspected, the family would consult a medium, who performs a "service", and a "meal" is offered to the upset spirit for the purpose of soothing its anger. In essence, the service or the meal's purpose is to mediate. Depending on the specific situation, sometimes drastic measures are required, to the extent of arranging a marriage for the upset spirit, if the spirit is "single" on the other side. Suitable single spirits will be recruited when this is necessary.

I actually don't know where I stand when it comes to this practice. One tends to seek hope from all sources when one is desperate. Due to the highly subjective nature of the practice, it opens a lot of doors for con-men to take advantage of such desperate minds. How do you prove that someone is ill because of the influence of some upset spirit? How do you prove the identity of the spirit? The medium will tell you who the offending party is, but is there any proof you can ask for? An X-ray? After multiple conversations with my friends and family, I am not sure if I can say this is a declining practice.

Spiritually Caught In Between

I learned of this story shortly after my arrival when I found out the details of the funeral arrangements of an aunt and an uncle (a couple) who passed away in the last few years. To tell the story, I have to give a little background information on religion. While the largest organized religion in Hong Kong is still Roman Catholicism, the most practiced religion is "ancestral worship." My extended family (a really large one!) generally practices this, even though some of us have turned to Christianity as we have grown up. In short, we believe that the deceased have some supernatural power over the descendants who survive them.

Anyway, I have two cousins who became very Christian, attended seminary and worked for the church. The whole nine yards. They felt the need to convert everyone in their family into Christians. Not with flying colors so far, I am afraid. Anyway, when their father, my uncle, was on his death bed, these said cousins succeeded in convincing the father to receive baptism so that his soul would be saved. The father passed away and the funeral, understandably, followed the Christian tradition.

Later on, my aunt repeatedly dreamt of my deceased uncle, who told her in her dreams that he was suffering in the other world. Specifically, according to my aunt, my uncle was stuck; he wasn't going up or going down and his spirit was suffering greatly. He asked her to give him a traditional "service" in which his soul could be sent to wherever it is that it belongs. The service took place, to the great dismay of my cousins, and the dreams stopped. As you can imagine, when my aunt was on her death bed, she was not about to receive baptism knowing what her deceased husband went through. She died without receiving baptism. To help her soul, my cousins gave her a Christian funeral the first night, followed by a more traditional Chinese funeral given by the other siblings the following night. No one has heard of her soul since the funeral.

This is a true story (as far as I know). Believe what you want. I respect other religions as long as they are fair and humane. I am not one to claim to have the "right" religion. As far as I am concerned, how one behaves "trumps" whom one believes any day.

51. Hangzhou, China - A City For Poets

August 4, 2005 – Hangzhou, China

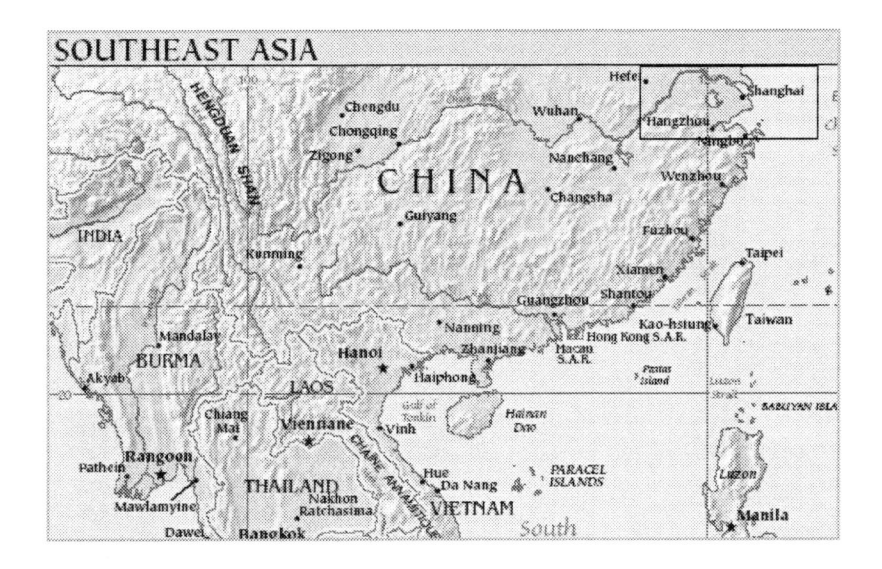

Hangzhou Bound

When I was in Hong Kong last October, a good friend of mine from college, Raina, and I casually talked about visiting her house in Hangzhou. On August 2, Raina, my 3rd sister Patty, her husband Four Eye Dragon, my soon-to-be-ten-year-old nephew Jacob and I caught the two hour Air China flight direct for Hangzhou. Hangzhou lies two hours southwest of Shanghai by train, about 90 miles away. When I was a tour guide in China in the eighties, I was always fond of this city because of its rich history, scenic surroundings, friendly people and relaxed lifestyle. Incidentally, this was the only city in China where I dared to ride a bike in those days. My last visit to this city was in 1988, eight years after China reopened her doors to the rest of the world. I didn't quite know what to expect this time around. Seventeen years made a world of difference in this part of the world.

Hangzhou - A City For Poets

This is definitely a city for poets. The history in this city goes back thousands of years. All Chinese students have studied prose and poems written in and/or about this place throughout the centuries. Legendary stories took place here, be they of war, politics, or love. According to the city's official site - "Hangzhou is one of the cradles of Chinese civilization. Human beings 4,700 years ago lived and prospered in this land, which is called 'Liangzhu Culture.' Hangzhou had once been the capital of the Wu and Yue kingdoms of the Five Dynasties during the 10th century and the capital of the Southern Song Dynasty during the 12th-13th centuries. It is one of the seven ancient Chinese capitals, famous for its historical and cultural heritage. The city has a history of more than 2200 years since it was established as a county by the First Emperor Qing."

Transportation

Transportation is the first thing that catches my attention. If you have seen any of the pictures or movies of China in the '80s or the early '90s, you would know that this country was full of bicycles. Nowadays, most of the bicycles have been replaced by automobiles. There are few bicycles these days by comparison. Those who can't afford an automobile opt for an electric bicycle. When fully charged, it travels about 15 kilometers (7 miles) per hour unassisted. The peddles are there, should the battery run out.

Our driver told me that automobiles are relatively affordable in China. They are made, guess where, in China. It is interesting to see Chinese characters on Honda, Toyota, Volkswagen, and Hyundai, to name a few. The only Chinese made American brand I have seen is GM, but they don't translate that into Chinese. Supposedly, the Shanghai factories have the best reputation, but the automobiles are made in multiple provinces. This is a huge market. Raina told me that during the SARS epidemic in 2003, many people who could afford to do so stayed away from public transportation and got behind the wheel instead. I don't want to even think about the environmental impact of this ever-increasing demand of fossil fuel.

China has begun to roll out its own domestic automobiles to compete with the imported brands. I read an article on the flight about this very matter. The article stated that it took Japan 40 years to make world-class automobiles; it took Korea half of that time. So, it is not entirely inconceivable whether it is possible for China to come up with world-class automobiles in a single decade. Only time can tell. Meanwhile, I am not too concerned about China's success on this matter; I am more interested in finding out where in the world we can get fossil fuel to support this kind of expansion.

In Hangzhou, it is good to see that the expansion does not create the kind of traffic jam that is commonplace in fast growing big cities. There are obvious plans to deal with the increasing traffic. However, traffic jams are still common in big cities like Shanghai, especially during rush hour.

Another thing that draws my attention is that the drivers are much more polite and civilized than they were in the past. This is a good sign as it indicates better civic education. One thing has not changed though. I was not able to cross the streets in China by myself seventeen years ago. It's a real test of your guts and judgment. I still can't do this. This week, I tried to cross the street in the city by myself and my knees went out on me when I was standing in the middle of the road, waiting for the next opportunity to get to the other side without getting myself killed.

I was afraid that the city's beauty, both internal and external, would be compromised for the sake of economic development. The principal attraction of the city is West Lake. I am pleased to report that the surroundings of the lake have been modernized, without losing their traditional charm.

Food Culture

Eating has always been a priority for the Chinese people. With the newly found consumption power, there are many eateries that cater to the demand of the people. Raina's father invited us to dinner in a restaurant. It featured 124 private spacious dining rooms. The place was so big that golf carts were used to transport the patrons from the entrance to their exclusive dining room. I visited the bathroom and was a bit surprised to find that it featured a small bamboo garden inside. I have never seen such a huge bathroom in my life. They told me that another restaurant of this kind was under construction in the same city and it featured 450 private dining rooms!

Serving portions have grown over the years and they now mirror those in America. Meat is a lot more common in a meal whereas traditionally vegetable was more common. Incidentally, I can definitely tell that the Chinese people are getting bigger (as in physical size) these days. In addition to the serving portions, I think the change from cycling to driving also has a lot to do with it. Helping people to lose weight is already a big business in Hong Kong, and it is quickly gaining popularity in mainland China. I must add that the Hong Kong people are not THAT big, but they are obsessed with being very skinny.

52. Other Observations In China

August 5, 2005 – Shanghai, China

Other Changes

There are many new residential and commercial developments in China. Hangzhou is a second tier class city. It's just very hard to imagine a country expanding at this rate economically. The farmers have done very well in this area as they lease their land to developers who build first-class homes for those who have made their fortune.

We went to a supermarket (not the largest one in town) in Hangzhou on a Sunday afternoon. There were 39 cashiers at the checkout point, each of which had a line of about 10 people waiting to pay. That's an eye opener for me. I spent most of the time browsing the electronics department. They sell mostly products made in China, including a large selection of oversized Plasma and LCD TVs. I appreciate the fact that they specify the very city where the product was assembled. Again, certain cities are perceived to have higher quality.

Another clue that I picked up about the improved economy (not that there is any shortage of visual reminders in the cities) is that people raise dogs as pets. Dogs were traditionally seen as being functional as security guard, and often times as food. They were seldom treated as companions, whereas nowadays many people have dogs as pets.

The entertainment industry fights pirating CDs and DVDs by lowering their prices for those products made in China. I bought about 20 music CDs, all fully copyrighted, for an average price of US$1.2 each. This kind of pricing strategy is effectively killing the pirate industry. Given that nobody was about to spend $10 on a CD, this is not a bad way to gain the market share. The volume itself is easily a 9-digit number in this country.

Mobile phones (cellular) are another huge business in this country. I couldn't imagine it until I saw the amount of advertisements and the number of people using cell phones. GSM being the standard, people can simply buy a new sim card and they get a cell number instantly. When we went to Shanghai, we forgot to bring Raina's cell phone from Hangzhou. When we got to Shanghai station, we found a store right next to the station and bought a card and inserted it in the phone we brought from Hong Kong. And voila! we were connected immediately.

Shanghai is the financial center for China and it is poised to rival London and New York one day. On the shopping scene, there are many world class shops - Gucci, Burberry, Bulgari, to name a few. Along with this rapid economic expansion comes the rising divorce rate. Divorce is no longer the taboo that it once was in the recent past. The divorce rate is, as expected, even higher in Hong Kong. But that's another subject. From what I see, China is more capitalistic than any other country I have known, with the possible exception of Hong Kong. Other than the political system, there's nothing communistic about this country. There's no womb-to-tomb government planning and there is no equality in wealth, health care, education, and the like as promised by classic communism. Make no mistake, I am neither complaining nor making a judgment call. I am just stating what I see.

Relationship With Taiwan - A Brief Glance

If you watch the news in the US, you would think that the relationship between China and Taiwan can only be characterized as being tense. Politically, it may be the case. What the US journalists don't have either the interest or the time to report is how the two people live. There are many Taiwanese investors in China, especially along the coastal cities. When I checked in for the return flight to Hong Kong, I was standing behind a group of Taiwanese tourists. The fact that the two countries share a common official language makes traveling on one's own easy.

There are more than 3,000 dialects in Chinese, and most of them are not mutually intelligible. As a result, Chinese people would never ask each other if they speak Chinese. Instead, they would ask if they speak a specific dialect such as Mandarin, Cantonese, Shanghaiese, Fukkinese, Hakka, etc. However, there is one written language, although there are the simplified forms (used in China) and the original forms (used in Taiwan and Hong Kong). Students are taught Mandarin in school as it is the official dialect in China. When two people come from two different regions (sometimes as close as 50 miles away, or even less, they may have two different dialects), and they have to use Mandarin to facilitate communications. However, not everyone is equally proficient in Mandarin, especially those who are less educated. Because of the many dialects used, most of the Chinese TV programs are subtitled in Chinese (I know it sounds funny), whether the dialog is in Mandarin or in a local dialect.

My friend's family has a dish for Taiwanese television programs. It features more than ten Taiwanese channels that specialize in news, movies, cartoons, variety shows, music, and so on. One interesting thing is that, in order to apply for the dish service, you have to show your "foreigner" status. Trust me, if one wants to, one can easily bypass that requirement. I don't know how myself, but I don't doubt the least bit that it can be done and that it has been done.

Speaking of television programs, the English news anchors (CCTV 9 - China Central TV) speak practically flawless English. This is quite a contrast from my experience in the late eighties. They also tend to prefer the American accent to the British version. I can only hope to acquire that kind of natural accent.

I think it is a good thing that the people (Chinese and Taiwanese) have such strong cultural and economic links among themselves. This kind of understanding will help ward off another civil war. The previous one brought the status of the two "countries." I personally consider them as two countries, but the Beijing government officially views Taiwan as a renegade province.

My prediction is that Taiwan will one day reunite with China, possibly following the model of Hong Kong and Macau. Unless China uses force to take Taiwan back, I don't see who in the world will step up to intervene. On what grounds do they intervene? And if China should use force, it would be unrealistic on the part of Taiwan to expect that the good old US of A will lend a helping hand. There simply is no spare military force to go around. After all, there is no oil in Taiwan to lure the lobbyists, and hence the current administration.

Pregnancy Permit

China is currently the most populous country in the world, boasting over 1,300 million. In an effort to control the population growth, China still enforces the one child system that was first put in place in the early 80s. However, it's slightly more lenient these days. Our driver in China educated me about the current practice.

Before I start, it is important to explain one basic policy about residence. When one is born, one's residence is registered in that region. Basically, all regions are further classified as being "urban" or "village", which is key when it comes to giving birth.

Before one gets pregnant, one "should" get a pregnancy permit, valid for 12 months, from the government. Understandably, a marriage certificate is required before the pregnancy permit can be granted. Without such permit, one will have a hard time getting medical attention when it's time for delivery. In practice, most married people wait until they are pregnant before they apply for the certificate, which renders the spirit of the permit void.

Unless both parents have "village" status, this is the only child that they can have. After giving birth, the woman is required to undergo a mandatory medical checkup every three months to make sure that she's not pregnant again. If the couple defies the law and proceeds to have a second child, they are subject to a fine of 2-4 times their annual salary. The salary is withheld directly from the payroll. In other words, if you can afford it, you can quit your job for 5 years to avoid the penalty entirely.

On the other hand, if both parents have "village" status, AND if the first child is a girl, they have the right to get pregnant for a second time after waiting for five years. Regardless of the gender of the second child, two is all they can have without subjecting themselves to a penalty.

On a related note, I learned that pre-marital sex among university students, be it on or off campus, is enough to subject individuals to being expelled from the university. This year, Shanghai Jiao Tung University, a prominent one in the country, proposes to remove that policy from its books to reflect the reality of the situation, or else 70% of the students will have to be kicked out among the universities throughout the country, according to a survey.

53. Follow-up To Previous Entry

August 12, 2005 – Hong Kong, China

On Marriage And Giving Birth

I forgot to mention two important things in my previous entry. First, the One Child Policy does not apply to the citizens of Hong Kong. They are free to have as many children as they would like. Many young couples are doing just that, and the favorite number of children is currently a big zero. Secondly, in China, the ever-increasing divorce rate makes it necessary for the government to specify how to determine whether a couple already has used its quota. The rules say that the quota goes with the mother. It's as simple as that and it leaves no room for interpretation.

This brings a few thoughts to my inquiring mind. I imagine that it will be, possibly significantly, more difficult for a single mother to walk down the aisle for a second time. That is, unless husband No. 2 is already a father through a previous marriage or he (or sometimes more importantly, his parents) doesn't care to continue his family name. Also, this is no easy market to look for a surrogate mother. Since homosexuality is a crime punishable by imprisonment and possibly more severely (not that it is enforced on a daily basis, the government is busy enough with promoting capitalism inside a communism framework,) there is little chance that the same-sex couples are openly shopping for surrogate mothers. Westerners flock to China to adopt baby girls; the Chinese couples can easily do the same should they have trouble getting pregnant. But what happens to the quota for those mothers who give up their baby for adoption? I really don't know.

I saw a huge ad in the paper and asked my sister what it meant. The title of the ad is "Single Man's Certificate". It is an ad from a law firm. Because of the increased cross border marriages, there needs to be a way to make sure that no one is married twice, as bigamy is prohibited by law in both China and Hong Kong. There are a lot more Hong Kong men marrying Chinese women and the reverse is still rare. Therefore, if you are interested in officially marrying a woman in China, you are required to prove that you are single. This law firm is one of those authorized to issue such a certificate.

A friend told me that the ratio between men and women, who are of marrying age and are single, is 3 to 7. Eventually, the women will have to cross the border (either to China or other countries) to look for a spouse. I see a huge business opportunity here.

I spent the weekend with a few buddies from high school. Walkins and his brother are both in a cross border marriage. His brother chose to work and live with his wife in China, while Walkins remains in Hong Kong and commutes to see his wife once every 2-3 weeks, not unlike a flying consultant would! My friends told me that the divorce rate is actually higher in China than it is in Hong Kong. Also, in spite of having lived under British rule for more than 100 years, Hong Kong people are comparatively more conservative than their counterparts in China, who came out of a closed society a brief twenty-five years ago. Nothing is ever as simple and straight forward as we think it anymore.

A Regional Oil Crisis

Speaking of China, recently there is a serious shortage of oil in the southern part of China across the border from Hong Kong. Starting last week - when oil prices started to skyrocket - a rationing was put in place and every car was only allowed to put in about $13 US worth of gas, and it was rumored to have been further lowered to half of that amount over the weekend. Considering the gas price is still roughly three times that of US, how far can you go with 2-3 gallons of gas? The taxi drivers do not get exempted either. On TV, they show long lines everywhere. Four thousand tons of oil are being shipped from the northern part of the country to ease the situation.

I think this particular crisis will be short-lived. However, like I stated earlier, this ever-increasing demand for fossil fuel in this gigantic country, along with India, will soon exceed what the earth's supply can meet. I really don't want to imagine the environmental impact. A hybrid car is looking more attractive by the day.

54. Fragrant Harbor III - Education

August 14, 2005 – Hong Kong, China

Education System In Hong Kong - A First Look

My brain is naturally wired to understand how education systems are structured. I had a good understanding of the educational system in the US before I ever stepped foot in that country. I learned how the Costa Rican system works while temporarily living there in the recent past.

I grew up and was educated in Hong Kong, yet I can't tell you with any certainty how the system works anymore. In April and May, form 5 (or equivalent to 11th graders) sat for an examination known as the Hong Kong Certificate of Education examination. They take a minimum of six subjects (the minimum number required to get a full certificate) and a maximum of up to 10 subjects. The exam results determine, though to less extent these days, the fate of those examined. Slightly less than 110,000 sat for the examination this year. The subjects ranged from Chinese, English, Mathematics, Chemistry, Physics, Art, Economics, Accounting to Technical Drawing and Metal Work, of which Chinese, English, and Mathematics are mandatory. If you score a certain point (14 is the number this year) in six subjects, you are guaranteed a spot in form 6 & 7 (12th & 13th grades). At the end of the 2 years, they sit for another exam which will determine whether they will be admitted by the local universities. This is the clearest explanation. Many who score less than 14 can still have a chance to get into form 6, but they have to wait according to their points, depending on the number of slots left unfilled.

When I finished high school more than 20 years ago, there were two degree-granting universities and only 2% of those in the 11th grade eventually entered a degree program. Yes, I was a reject and I am not (very) bitter! Right now, there are seven universities, all public or heavily subsidized. More than 20% of the 11th graders will enter one of these universities locally. In addition to form 6, there is a plethora of outlets for those who don't or who aren't qualified to follow this path. There are vocational institutes and there are many private schools. There are two groups of private schools: the very bad ones and the very rich and good ones (using the single criterion of tier one university admission). You can easily tell which ones are which by the price tag. The good ones are touted as being "international," following the curriculum of the country they market under. Australia, Canada, America are a few of them. Their tuition and fees rival those of private universities in the US. For me, the educational system in Hong Kong succinctly epitomizes the society it finds itself in. Most people here would agree that the educational system is sickly. Though, I imagine less of them feel that the society is as sickly.

A week ago, a friend relayed a conversation he had to me. If you do a survey among the top 100 government officials, you will find that only an insignificant amount among their own offspring will remain in Hong Kong for higher education. This distinctly reminds me that only one US Congress member has a child in active duty in Iraq - and these are the very people who are sending others' children to war. A close parallel, though much more lethal. There's little wonder that the educational system is where it is.

Also, those very good students (defined as scoring really high on these examinations; this year, 10 students got 10 As, or they scored the top 1-2% in the subjects being tested, a near impossible mission) choose internationally renowned institutions in Europe or North America over the local colleges. The result is that the local colleges have to allure top students from mainland China by offering them full scholarship and such, as a remedy to the ever-declining standard.

I understand that education is a business, and when an institute is not run like a business, it is destined for closure. In fact, education is an extremely big business worldwide, but here it manages to sound more like a business than education. And the disguise is surprisingly thin.

What has become very popular over the last 10 years is for foreign universities to offer their degree programs locally. Yes, you can get a UK, US or Australian degree without ever getting on a plane. These are NOT distance learning programs. They are instructor led. The universities run these programs in conjunction with a local institute and, 2-3 years later, voila!, you hold a degree that grants you all the privileges and rights as someone who has been attending the school on campus. The programs tend to concentrate on Business subjects (no need for much infrastructural investment). The government, when it comes to employment, recognizes some of the qualifications of these graduates. It publishes a list of the schools that it recognizes. When it comes to the private sector, it's fair game.

For me, the real confusion comes from high school admission programs. In fact, it is so complicated that I wouldn't even bother to start to describe it. Let's just say that it is not unusual for 5th or 6th graders (those who come from families with financial resources) to have portfolios and they use these portfolios to get into the high school of their choice. The portfolios highlight their special skills that their targeted high school may find attractive to be included in the school. This includes experience in drama, piano, a classical Chinese instrument, Chinese opera, kung fu, and so on. Incidentally, the "best" high schools are not private; they are public or semi-public, and the government pays the churches or other groups to run the school on its behalf. And, competition for the sought after schools can be fierce, to put it mildly. My friends tried to explain that to me, and for the life of me, I couldn't fully understand or remember all the details involved. All I remember from that conversation is that life is too short for such relentless competition.

55. Fragrant Harbor IV - Katrina Talk

September 14, 2005 – Hong Kong, China

Typhoons (Hurricanes In The Pacific)

It has been a month since my previous journal entry. A lot has happened around the world and there was so much to write about, but I chose the easy way out and my brain went on vacation from the site instead. It is high time I caught up with these journal entries before this sabbatical ends later this month. The year-long travel, the heat, the humidity, the disastrous world news, and the opening of the Hong Kong Disneyland (one is bombarded by it 24/7 with its unrelenting publicity) finally did me in and I spent the month doing what I needed to do most - nothing.

There has been an increased number of typhoons, and they have hit Taiwan and coastal China multiple times this summer. The effect on the temperature and air pressure has been most uncomfortable. The truth is that I have been under the weather for a few weeks. In fact, my condition prompted me to cancel a planned trip to Japan. It turned out to be a good thing as Japan was hit by a typhoon during that time. I went to see a doctor, and he reassured me that I am basically very healthy. I resorted to a Chinese herbal medicine practitioner. The doctor prescribed some extremely bitter herbal "soup." It seems to help.

During the last month, I visited families and friends, which automatically translates into eating. While my friends comment that every time they have seen me since my arrival, I have been steadily gaining weight. They keep feeding me, saying that I won't get to eat this well for another year. Lacking self discipline, I am afraid that social activities have become a health hazard for me here. The serving portions in Hong Kong have grown quite a bit over the last few years. They also have started to resemble those of North America. Hong Kong's weight management companies, diet plans and medication, and availability of fitness centers rival their counterparts in America in quantity. Meanwhile, the people are also subtly gaining weight. The people are mostly considered skinny by western standards, but I see subtle changes when compared with my previous visits nonetheless. Obesity is not a problem in Hong Kong. Not yet. However, that problem is quickly becoming serious in the developed cities in China.

Katrina - A Disaster Behind A Beautiful Name

I watched the local news (yes, it is a major news item here, just behind, you guessed it right, Hong Kong Disneyland) and heard comments that it's a national disgrace. Well, I got to experience this disgrace from afar. I don't intend to add to the criticisms of how the current administration and the local governments have handled the disaster. Other than Mr. Rush Limbaugh, few have anything good to say. Neither do I. My friends and family, of course, asked my "American" opinion of the event and they wanted me to confirm if racial discrimination is a big problem in the States. The images on TV and the commentaries prompted such an inquiry. Understandably.

Regarding racism, I have to say that I haven't experienced it personally, but then I tend to be rather ditzy about this kind of thing. So, if it happened to me, I probably didn't even realize it. Having said that, I would find it difficult to imagine that it doesn't exist in any society. Personally, I think the big problem in America, as in much of the world, especially in China in the coming years, is the gap between the "haves" and the "have-nots." This extreme uneven distribution of wealth is a real time bomb in America. Even though China has been experiencing unprecedented growth in the last two decades, more than 900 million of her people live below the poverty line as set out by the United Nations, according to one report that I came across. However, if you visit only the large Chinese cities, you would never believe that. The poor and the underprivileged tend to be conveniently hidden from the casual eyes. Out of sight; out of mind.

I overheard an interesting conversation on the bus the other day when I went to Discovery Bay, a resort style residential area, with its private beach. Because it's removed from the more central but more crowded area of the city, this place has long been a favorite among the expatriates who live in Hong Kong. I was at the back of the bus and the air-conditioner was making a lot of noise and was not functioning at full capacity. The few Chinese ladies around me made a comment that unless the foreigners make a complaint, the bus company will not take this bus out of service and do the necessary repairs.

In essence, there are two kinds of racial discrimination going on in Hong Kong. The city has a lot of live-in maids from the Philippines, Thailand, and Indonesia. It also has a lot of new immigrants from mainland China. I would say that these two groups are being discriminated against, though to different extents and for different reasons - the former group for their social status and darker complexion; the latter group for their "je ne sais quoi." Then, there is the reverse discrimination. Hong Kong being a British colony for so many years, most of the high government positions were held by the British who immigrated to Hong Kong from the UK. Over the years, people have subconsciously learned to defer to the Anglos, be they British, American, Australian, German, and so on and so forth. Part of it has to do with the language. The reverse discrimination still exists (it's easier to address the complaints by doing whatever is requested, right or wrong, than to reason and argue with someone in a foreign language), but it's less so these days.

Speaking of the expatriates, I went to the financial district one evening for dinner and observed that the Anglos are VERY different from my friends in America. I couldn't quite put a finger on it. When I told my friend at dinner about this, a native Texan who has been living in Hong Kong for five years, he said that they look unapproachable and he doesn't hang out with them either. That's what it is.

56. Fragrant Harbor V - Public Transportation

September 16, 2005 – Hong Kong, China

I Am In Hong Kong, But I Am Not Sure If I Am At Home

Ever since my arrival, I wonder if I would feel at home again after a few weeks. I didn't exactly know how that feeling could be measured. One day this week, it dawned on me that I still feel like a visitor. I say so for a few reasons. Firstly, language-wise, there is a noticeable amount of new popular slang that my friends have to explain to me. There was a change in the use of a certain word that I still can't get used to. Every time people use the word this way (even the news anchors use it), it sounds wrong to my ears - as in "irregardless" - if I must give it an English equivalent. Secondly, I cannot get over how surprised and impressed I am about the efficiency of the public transportation. I invariably pick the front seat on the upper deck of the double deck buses to get the best view. The locals have the sense that this might be the worst seat to be in if a rare collision should happen. Finally, the telecommunications industry amazes me with its offerings at dirt-cheap prices. I think I am impressed by all these things partially because I subconsciously keep comparing these things with the last city where I used the system extensively - San Jose, Costa Rica.

Public Transportation

The fact that there is a large number of people living in such a small place requires a good public transportation system. Hong Kong is the only big city that I know where the traffic improves instead of worsens by the year. In fact, the traffic has improved to the point that, in this city, you can feasibly live anywhere regardless of where your job is. Almost. There are some smaller inhabited islands that depend totally on ferry services.

There is a plethora of public transportation to choose from. The Mass Transit Railway (MTR) moves more than 2.25 million people a day - it has six lines, including one Airport Express that takes you from the airport (very remotely located) to the heart of the financial district in only 23 minutes. The Kowloon Canton Railway (KCR) runs three lines connecting the New Territories to the city - all with interchanges with the MTR. There are a number of bus companies - most of them offer double deck services and, with the exception of a handful of routes, all buses are air-conditioned. Bus services are available in a large part of the city 24 hours a day.

There is a light rail in the New Territories that connects a number of towns. The tram - my favorite by far - is the second oldest and still runs east-west on the Hong Kong Island. The tram tracks were built along the harbor, but land reclamation over the last hundred years kept moving the waterfront further out into the harbor and the tram tracks are practically inland these days. The oldest public transportation system in the city is the Peak Tram that takes one from the foothill to the Victoria Peak. An exciting ride. Then there are mini buses and taxis. Of course, ferry services connect the offshore islands as well as Hong Kong Island with the peninsula.

Part of the improvements came from the construction and expansion of the MTR and KCR systems. The government has been investing heavily in improving the infrastructure by building a number of bridges, tunnels, and highways as well as improving the interchange points so that changing from one highway to another is seamless. There are also strict rules by which one can park curbside and one can load and unload. This week, the gas price is HK$13.23 a liter, or roughly US$6.4 a gallon. Parking is expensive although parking spaces have been made more available in recent years. A very large majority of the people in this city use public transportation. Even people who own cars mostly avoid driving during the week.

To illustrate my point, I stay with my sister in Lantau by the new airport and I travel to visit my parents frequently. Before 1997, if I were to make this trip, I would have to take a bus to the pier, and then take a ferry, then the MTR, and then another bus ride. The whole thing takes at least four hours, if I make all the connections without having to wait more than 5-10 minutes. Nowadays, thanks to a series of new bridges and tunnels, a one-hour bus ride separates the two points. No need to change at all. And it is air-conditioned. If I had made this trip before 1980 (the year Phase I of MTR was put in service), I would have, no doubt, packed a change of clothes!

Octopus - The System That Makes A Cashless Society Possible

Hong Kong devised a charging system called Octopus. It's a card that you prepay (at the subway stations or any 7-Eleven in the city, or through automatic bank transfers), and you can use it for almost all public transportations, even though they are owned by different companies - except taxis and some of the mini buses. The beauty of the Octopus is that there's no need for the driver to count money and to make change. Before the Octopus, one must prepare the exact fare, and the driver had to verify if the payment was right.

The card itself is like the security card that is popular in many office buildings. You place the card on the pad (reader) and it identifies who you are. With the card, it deducts the right amount from your available balance when you board the bus. You scan the card when you enter the subway, and you scan it when you exit. The amount deducted is based on the distance traveled. All automatic. You don't even have to take the card out. You can simply keep the card in your wallet and place the wallet on the reader. Most ladies keep their cards inside the purses (at or near the bottom) and they just place the whole purse on the reader. It works like charm.

You can also use this card in many stores, like 7-Eleven, food courts, and the supermarkets, to name a few. It's a lot faster than credit cards as there's need to wait for approval and a signature. Deduction is quick (one second or even less) and accurate. You can also use it in vending machines. You save yourself a lot of frustration when you are out of coins and dying of thirst!

Some apartment buildings integrate their security systems with the Octopus. The same card that allows you to travel around the city and shop in many places also allows you access to your building. There's no need to carry additional cards. A high school requires the students to register their attendance by placing their Octopus on the reader at the entrance of the school. This way, the school instantly knows who has arrived to school without carrying out any head counts!

To top it, the Octopus also comes in the form of watches. That's the kind that I use. My fully functioning watch is also my Octopus. This is the perfect solution for me as I don't even have to reach for my wallet when boarding a bus or the subway.

This Octopus thing was invented in Hong Kong and it is being exported to other countries and cities in the region. It truly enables a cashless society.

57. The Fat Lady Has Sung

December 27, 2005 – Dallas, Texas

The fat lady has sung; it is over.

What Took So Long?

More than 70,000 words, 2,500 photos and 10 countries later, this fantastic journey has finally reached its end. I had been working on the draft of this final entry for almost three months and not much progress was made. Eventually, I had to examine within me what caused such sluggishness. The answer finally came to me this morning.

I realized that, subconsciously, I did not want this sabbatical to end. Like I said in my annual newsletter 2005, this is one of the most wonderful years of my life. And I have had some good ones in the past, if I may be so bold to say so. In addition, it was a lot of work to get back to reality. I went back to work and resumed the commuting lifestyle four days after returning from Hong Kong. To further complicate things, I signed the paper on a condo a few days later. Having said all that, the truth be known, I am just not the most efficient/effective person I know. Case in point, I started reading Stephen R. Covey's *7 Habits of Highly Effective People* back in 2000, and the bookmark has not been able to move beyond the 3rd habit yet. I came to the conclusion that I may never be effective enough to learn all the 7 habits after all.

(Some Of The) Lessons Learned

I have only been taking mental notes on the lessons that I have learned on this journey. Here are some of them. Allow me to point out that this is not meant to sound like a sermon. I do not claim any universal truth in them. These are simply, as the subtitle above suggests, the lessons I learned from this sabbatical, and they are my personal views.

Life Is Very Short

Time flies. I saw it happening in front of my eyes. I spent a whole year on the road. When it was over, it felt like a month. Only when I recount what I have done during the year do I emotionally realize that I did take a year off. I saw that, on the average, people are much more careful with their money than they are with their time, i.e. their lives. I learned that I need to have a better awareness of the fact that life is a gift that can be taken away at any given moment. While I need to plan for the future, it is equally important to live in the present. Incidentally, in my travels, I saw that a lot of people are aiming for the quantity of life, but not the quality of life.

A year went by quickly, and so did the first 40 years of my life. I must confess that I have no solid idea how the next 40 (one can hope) will fare. I do know this: whatever it is that I do, I shall not take it for granted.

Live My Own Dreams

I only let a few people know of my plan to take a year off until a few months before the sabbatical started. I was afraid that people would react negatively to the plan and that I would end up having to defend it. It turned out that most people were very supportive, even though some of them were convinced that I had completely lost my mind this time. One friend specifically questioned if it was possible for me to live a year without structure. Others were afraid that I would not be able to get my job back when the year was over. These were all legitimate concerns, but the temptation of living in Central America and acquiring the Spanish language was too great to let the opportunity pass.

Now that it is over, I am glad that none of these concerns stopped me from pursuing this dream. Taking a year-long sabbatical was truly the best gift I could have given myself for my fortieth birthday. The best thing about this gift is that I don't need any warranty or guarantee as no matter what happens from now on, nothing can take that away from me.

I was surprised by the number of people that expressed their desire to do something similar, especially the taking-a-year-off part. I truly hope that one day they get to experience what it is like to be free of obligations for an extended period of time, before they retire. During this year, I got to be Andy Pang the person, not Andy Pang the consultant or whatever title/designation that may follow the name. It was a most liberating experience. I once read a quote that said, "A lot of people want to live a long life, and yet most of them don't know what to do with themselves on a rainy Sunday afternoon." Now I know what I would do, for I have had a year of rainy Sunday afternoons!

Life Is Not A Competition

Along the line of living my own dreams, I also learned not to compare myself with others. I am lucky to have a lot of friends who do much better than I do in many areas of life. If I readily allow myself to be compared with them, then I will fall in the trap of living their dreams. However, if I choose to make the things that they excel in part of my dreams, then these people should become my inspiration instead. To turn these things into a source for my sense of inadequacy would be a total waste of the gift that they can be in my life.

I learned that I want to live, not merely exist. When I die, I want my headstone to read "Here lies Andy Pang. He was a good friend." In three languages - English, Chinese and Spanish. Oops, my living will says that I want to be cremated. Oh well, they will just have to use a very small font on the mail-box-sized niche in the columbarium where they will keep my ashes.

Life's Equality And Inequality

Life is NOT fair. This is especially true for those of us who happen to live in the "first world." The truth of the matter is that we drew the long straw, and by far. The fact that you are able to read, and that you are reading this online, easily puts you in the top 10% across the human spectrum. Ironically, it doesn't make us automatically happier people. Often, all we can see is what is absent in our lives, rather than the abundance. I have seen some very poor standards of living this year. Make no mistake, being poor doesn't automatically make people happier either.

One is invariably miserable if the basic necessities are not met - shelter, food, clothes, security, etc. Once these are met, the road to happiness takes a detour. Material things, both tangible and intangible, can fill the void only to an extent and only for a limited time. I learn that material things are neutral in themselves. They are neither good nor bad. They just are. How I relate to material things is what makes a world of difference. I have met as many happy "poor" people as I have unhappy "rich" people. And vice versa. I realize that life is fair, however, in that happiness comes from within. And, to a very large extent, we are in full control of it, if we should choose to do so.

It is ironic that the people who work the hardest are often the ones who need the money the least, as in the fact that they will not go hungry or homeless if they should work less and strike for more of a work/life balance.

Having said all this, I do believe that the world's biggest threat is the rapidly growing gap between the rich and the poor. The rich are getting richer while the poor seem to be getting ever poorer. I see that this is happening in the richest countries as well as the poorest countries. One of the few possible exceptions is my beloved Denmark.

Back To Reality

Coming back to reality is scarily easy in terms of resuming my work life. However, the logistics of resuming a normal life were equally, if not more, complicated as when I left this life a year ago.

Coming back to America was welcoming and somewhat difficult at the same time. I am glad to see that things function the way I have grown accustomed to. Toilets work and most things can be arranged via a phone call or the internet. Meanwhile, having been away for a year makes me more sensitive to some of the madness that is going on in my adopted country. To that end, so far, I have opted not to have a television set in my new home. In this case, ignorance is a blessing for me. I was not born here, but I made a conscious choice to be a citizen of this country several years ago. This makes me an insider and an outsider at the same time. At times, this disparity inevitably gives me a different perspective on this country from some of my fellow citizens who were born here.

These days, my main connection to the world is National Public Radio and BBC, and whatever USA Today finds fit to print during the week when I am on the road. The unexpected benefit of this decision of not having a TV set is that it allows me more time to reconnect with old acquaintances, to make some new friends, and to contemplate on what the next milestone birthday shall bring.

58. Epilogue

December 28, 2005 – Dallas, Texas

I confess that, at the beginning of the sabbatical, having seen a lot of semi-abandoned personal websites, I was highly skeptical whether I would have the interest and perseverance to maintain the website for a whole year. Indeed, it is surprising that it turned out to be a prolific year for me in cyberspace.

There is a large number of people that have helped make this sabbatical happen. I have a lot of people to thank and I am sure I have forgotten to include some in this list. If I have forgotten you, you know who you are and your kindness was not taken for granted. Here are some of them (in no specific order):

Costa Rica

Alvaro & Gilberto & Dona Claudina - for housing and feeding me in Costa Rica and for throwing me my 3rd birthday party of the year;

Alonso - for the friendship whenever I felt "out of place" in Costa Rica;

Gaby, Luis and their three kids - for giving me a sense of connectedness in Costa Rica;

Vida Abundante & Renacer Esperanza - for taking me into their organizations, giving me the opportunity to serve with them and to experience life among them in their communities;

United States

Helen & Vance (aka my southern parents) and *Diane & Dick* (aka my west coast parents) - for their love, accommodation and encouragement, and their mental assurance that I wouldn't be homeless on my return, should I fail to find a job quickly;

Neal - for keeping my car and making sure that the battery didn't die, all the scheduled maintenance, the unsolicited waxing of the car!;

Maurice - for driving 40 miles each week to take care of my mail and repeatedly providing logistical support, and for visiting me in Costa Rica;

Bob, Mike - for accommodating me during my interim visits to Dallas and throwing me an unforgettable 40th birthday party;

Keith - for allowing me to camp out on his couch and turn his dining room into my temporary office towards the end of the sabbatical and before I moved into my own space;

Jim, Jerry - for accommodating me during my interim visits to Dallas;

Alicia (my Texmex sister) - for helping me to move out of my apartment;

Tom B. - for the kind and encouraging words and timely assurances throughout the year that I actually hadn't lost my mind;

Belinda - for always being there and those long distance calls;

Prof. Mark - for generously agreeing to edit the book that results from this website;

Dude - for teaching me everything I know about maintaining a website;

Mr. Pounds at Solbourne Computers - for allowing me to take a sabbatical; my friends just could not believe that my boss is understanding (and somehow crazy) enough to go with the idea;

Hong Kong

My sister Patty and her husband Four-Eye Dragon - for giving me free food and accommodation for 10 weeks in Hong Kong;

My younger brother Tim - for letting me use his new home to get some rare moments of solitude in Hong Kong;

Raina - for hosting me in her home in Hangzhou for a week and showing me her beautiful hometown;

Vegas - for his logistics support and for being my personal "Kinkos" in Hong Kong;

Denmark

Vibeke & Ole (aka my Danish parents) - for accommodating me in Denmark and throwing me my first 40th birthday party.

The World

YOU - many thanks to those of you who let me know that my words were indeed read (so, I'd better watch out about what I am saying?) and the photos were viewed. Your words were the source of energy that kept this website going for a year.

Appendix

Calendar

First Quarter

October 2004

Mon	Tue	Wed	Thu	Fri	Sat	Sun
				1 Dallas	2 Dallas	3 Dallas
4 Dallas	5 Dallas	6 Air	7 Hong Kong	8 Hong Kong	9 Hong Kong	10 Hong Kong
11 Hong Kong	12 Hong Kong	13 Hong Kong	14 Hong Kong	15 Hong Kong	16 Hong Kong	17 Hong Kong
18 Dallas	19 Dallas	20 Dallas	21 Dallas	22 Dallas	23 London	24 London
25 London	26 London	27 London	28 London	29 London	30 London	31 London

November 2004

Mon	Tue	Wed	Thu	Fri	Sat	Sun
1 London	2 London	3 London	4 London	5 London	6 London	7 London
8 London	9 London	10 London	11 London	12 London	13 London	14 London
15 London	16 London	17 London	18 London	19 London	20 Denmark	21 Denmark
22 Denmark	23 Denmark	24 Denmark	25 London	26 Dallas	27 Dallas	28 Dallas
29 Dallas	30 Costa Rica	1 Costa Rica	2 Costa Rica	3 Costa Rica	4 Costa Rica	5 Costa Rica

December 2004

Mon	Tue	Wed	Thu	Fri	Sat	Sun
6 Costa Rica	7 Costa Rica	8 Costa Rica	9 Costa Rica	10 Costa Rica	11 Costa Rica	12 Costa Rica
13 Costa Rica	14 Costa Rica	15 Costa Rica	16 Costa Rica	17 Panama	18 Panama	19 Panama
20 Panama	21 Panama	22 Panama	23 Panama	24 Panama	25 Panama	26 Panama
27 Panama	28 Panama	29 Panama	30 Costa Rica	31 Costa Rica	1 Costa Rica	2 Costa Rica

210 | Life's Scenic Lookout

Second Quarter

January 2005

Mon	Tue	Wed	Thu	Fri	Sat	Sun
27 Panama	28 Panama	29 Panama	30 Costa Rica	31 Costa Rica	1 Costa Rica	2 Costa Rica
3 Costa Rica	4 Costa Rica	5 Costa Rica	6 Costa Rica	7 Costa Rica	8 Costa Rica	9 Costa Rica
10 Costa Rica	11 Costa Rica	12 Costa Rica	13 Costa Rica	14 Costa Rica	15 Costa Rica	16 Costa Rica
17 Costa Rica	18 Costa Rica	19 Costa Rica	20 Costa Rica	21 Costa Rica	22 Costa Rica	23 Costa Rica
24 Costa Rica	25 Costa Rica	26 Costa Rica	27 Costa Rica	28 Costa Rica	29 Costa Rica	30 Costa Rica

February 2005

Mon	Tue	Wed	Thu	Fri	Sat	Sun
31 Costa Rica	1 Costa Rica	2 Costa Rica	3 Costa Rica	4 Costa Rica	5 Costa Rica	6 Costa Rica
7 Costa Rica	8 Costa Rica	9 Costa Rica	10 Costa Rica	11 Dallas	12 Dallas	13 Dallas
14 Dallas	15 Dallas	16 Dallas	17 Birmingham	18 Birmingham	19 Birmingham	20 Dallas
21 Miami	22 Costa Rica	23 Costa Rica	24 Costa Rica	25 Costa Rica	26 Costa Rica	27 Costa Rica
28 Costa Rica						

March 2005

Mon	Tue	Wed	Thu	Fri	Sat	Sun
28 Costa Rica	1 Costa Rica	2 Costa Rica	3 Costa Rica	4 Costa Rica	5 Costa Rica	6 Costa Rica
7 Costa Rica	8 Costa Rica	9 Costa Rica	10 Costa Rica	11 Costa Rica	12 Costa Rica	13 Costa Rica
14 Costa Rica	15 Costa Rica	16 Costa Rica	17 Costa Rica	18 Costa Rica	19 Costa Rica	20 Costa Rica
21 Costa Rica	22 Costa Rica	23 Costa Rica	24 Costa Rica	25 Costa Rica	26 Costa Rica	27 Costa Rica
28 Costa Rica	29 Costa Rica	30 Costa Rica	31 Costa Rica	1 Costa Rica	2 Costa Rica	3 Costa Rica

Third Quarter

April 2005

Mon	Tue	Wed	Thu	Fri	Sat	Sun
28 Costa Rica	29 Costa Rica	30 Costa Rica	31 Costa Rica	1 Costa Rica	2 Costa Rica	3 Costa Rica
4 Costa Rica	5 Costa Rica	6 Costa Rica	7 Costa Rica	8 Costa Rica	9 Costa Rica	10 Costa Rica
11 Costa Rica	12 Costa Rica	13 Costa Rica	14 Costa Rica	15 Costa Rica	16 Costa Rica	17 Costa Rica
18 Costa Rica	19 Costa Rica	20 Costa Rica	21 Costa Rica	22 Costa Rica	23 Dallas	24 Dallas
25 Dallas	26 Dallas	27 Dallas	28 Dallas	29 Dallas	30 Dallas	1 Dallas

May 2005

Mon	Tue	Wed	Thu	Fri	Sat	Sun
2 Ft. Lauderdale	3 Caribbean	4 San Juan	5 St. Thomas	6 St. Lucia	7 Martinique	8 Barbados
9 Atlantic Ocean	10 Atlantic Ocean	11 Atlantic Ocean	12 Atlantic Ocean	13 Atlantic Ocean	14 Funchal, Madeiras	15 Atlantic Ocean
16 Malaga, Spain	17 Mediterranean	18 Barcelona	19 Genoa, Italy	20 Dallas	21 Dallas	22 Dallas
23 Costa Rica	24 Costa Rica	25 Costa Rica	26 Costa Rica	27 Costa Rica	28 Costa Rica	29 Costa Rica

June 2005

Mon	Tue	Wed	Thu	Fri	Sat	Sun
30 Costa Rica	31 Costa Rica	1 Costa Rica	2 Costa Rica	3 Costa Rica	4 Costa Rica	5 Costa Rica
6 Costa Rica	7 Costa Rica	8 Costa Rica	9 Costa Rica	10 Costa Rica	11 Costa Rica	12 Costa Rica
13 Costa Rica	14 Costa Rica	15 Costa Rica	16 Costa Rica	17 Costa Rica	18 Costa Rica	19 Costa Rica
20 Costa Rica	21 Costa Rica	22 Costa Rica	23 Costa Rica	24 Costa Rica	25 Costa Rica	26 Costa Rica
27 Costa Rica	28 Costa Rica	29 Costa Rica	30 Costa Rica	1 Dallas	2 Dallas	3 Dallas

Fourth Quarter

July 2005

Mon	Tue	Wed	Thu	Fri	Sat	Sun
27 Costa Rica	28 Costa Rica	29 Costa Rica	30 Costa Rica	1 Dallas	2 Dallas	3 Dallas
4 Dallas	5 Dallas	6 Birmingham	7 Birmingham	8 Birmingham	9 Birmingham	10 Birmingham
11 Dallas	12 Los Angeles	13 Los Angeles	14 Air	15 Hong Kong	16 Hong Kong	17 Hong Kong
18 Hong Kong	19 Hong Kong	20 Hong Kong	21 Hong Kong	22 Hong Kong	23 Hong Kong	24 Hong Kong
25 Hong Kong	26 Hong Kong	27 Hong Kong	28 Hong Kong	29 Hong Kong	30 Hong Kong	31 Hong Kong

August 2005

Mon	Tue	Wed	Thu	Fri	Sat	Sun
1 Hong Kong	2 Hangzhou, China	3 Hangzhou, China	4 Shanghai	5 Shanghai	6 Hangzhou, China	7 Hangzhou, China
8 Hangzhou, China	9 Hong Kong	10 Hong Kong	11 Hong Kong	12 Hong Kong	13 Hong Kong	14 Hong Kong
15 Hong Kong	16 Hong Kong	17 Hong Kong	18 Hong Kong	19 Hong Kong	20 Hong Kong	21 Hong Kong
22 Hong Kong	23 Hong Kong	24 Hong Kong	25 Hong Kong	26 Hong Kong	27 Hong Kong	28 Hong Kong
29 Hong Kong	30 Hong Kong	31 Hong Kong	1 Hong Kong	2 Hong Kong	3 Hong Kong	4 Hong Kong

September 2005

Mon	Tue	Wed	Thu	Fri	Sat	Sun
5 Hong Kong	6 Hong Kong	7 Hong Kong	8 Hong Kong	9 Hong Kong	10 Hong Kong	11 Hong Kong
12 Hong Kong	13 Hong Kong	14 Hong Kong	15 Hong Kong	16 Hong Kong	17 Hong Kong	18 Hong Kong
19 Hong Kong	20 Hong Kong	21 Hong Kong	22 Dallas	23 Dallas	24 Dallas	25 Dallas
26	-	-	Back to Work		-	

ISBN 1412086899-2